Slow Escapes

RURAL RETREATS FOR CONSCIOUS TRAVELERS

gestalten

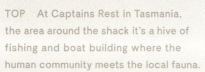

002

TOP   At Captains Rest in Tasmania, the area around the shack it's a hive of fishing and boat building where the human community meets the local fauna.

ABOVE   Nest 13 offers contemplative breaks overlooking the landscape of the Schaalsee Biosphere Reserve in northern Mecklenburg, Germany, with its extensive fields and meadows, wide horizons, and majestic beech forests.

ABOVE   At Morgado do Quintão, a landmark vineyard and farmstay in Portugal's Algarve, a passion for the land and food merges with a love of local heritage.

IN PRAISE OF
A NEW FORM OF RURALITY

INTRODUCTION

Slow Escapes explores a new generation of hotels, guesthouses, and hospitality venues that have traded the bustle of cities for the peace of remote and regional areas. Combining slow living with responsible tourism, these rural retreats are engaging with the land, revitalizing communities, and helping preserve culture and tradition—all through a new kind of travel.

Many dream of going back to nature, of breathing deeply and slowing down, of waking at sunrise to the sound of birdsong, feeling refreshed and replenished. To many city dwellers, stressed and drained by an urban environment that prioritizes speed and performance, this vision seems unattainable. Yet, the desire to get back to basics, to live in a sustainable way close to nature and closer to ourselves is on the rise. Faced with the increasing complexity of the modern world, there is a growing need for places that provide a sense of refuge. Going back to nature and visiting rural areas do just that. Both seem to hold the key to a new way forward and sit at the heart of this new movement in hospitality.

A different kind of vacation destination is emerging, one outside of cities that respects and celebrates rural areas. Located in remote places with a strong connection to nature, these venues are the antithesis of the loud, busy, and all too visible resorts of old. Merging with the landscape and embracing the community, they are run by dedicated individuals, many of whom have themselves left busy lives of "doing," to embrace a local, rural way of "being." These places and the people behind them empower local communities through employment and engagement, but they also

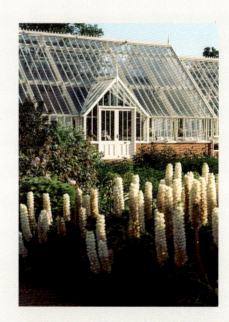

ABOVE   The glass house and upper walled garden at Heckfield Place, Hampshire, UK.

ABOVE The ancient town of Polignano a Mare, a 30-minute drive from Masseria Calderisi in Puglia, Italy.

learn from them. They work with local artisans and craftspeople, they embrace traditions—both the culinary and the cultural—and by working toward a new future they reinvigorate the past. Driven by authenticity, they support communities by promoting care and shared moments. Sustainable in the way they are built and run, these new rural escapes embrace their immediate surroundings, creating a real, seasonal sense of place and lasting change for those who spend time there.

The popularity of such ventures comes at a time when many regional and rural areas are experiencing significant depopulation—a problem created by the postindustrial landscape and lack of prospects that come with it. People born in small rural towns often leave in search of education and employment, a necessary act that only perpetuates the depopulation of rural areas, creating aging communities and decreasing economic dynamism as a result. When handled in a conscious, considerate manner, tourism can help reinvigorate such places by providing economic and social opportunities for the community. The "new rurals," an offshoot of the slow movement, are one such example of this.

The concept of slow tourism appeared in the wake of slow food, a movement about growing, preparing, and eating local produce that focuses not only on nutrition but on how food can help preserve culture and tradition. Similar principles were transposed to travel: people began to refuse mass tourism because of the way that it exhausts resources. Little by little, the movement changed the way we take vacations: closer to home in a more conscious manner; the way that we work: very often remotely; the clothes we buy: fewer, because we repair, reuse, and recycle; and the cosmetics we use: choosing naturally sourced over chemicals.

With control over their time, followers of the slow movement refuse the performance ideal. Valuing experience over consumption, they want to spend more time outside and together with friends and loved ones. They give back, getting involved with the local community or in actions to protect the environment because living sustainably is at the core of their daily lives. Concerned about climate change, they are strongly opposed to the consumerism and materialist principles that ruled their parents' lives. In a world that is already sick, they value and embrace the urgent need to slow down for nature, for biodiversity, and for humans to heal. Leading more balanced lives, they garden, cook, make, mend, and share.

What these conscious travelers have brought to the hospitality industry is immense. First, the way of life they promote impacted hoteliers: as guests they had more grounding needs, they looked for rural destinations close to nature, they asked for bikes and were keen to forage or visit animals on the property, they wanted to participate as well as meditate, and were open to vegetarian dishes only. A decade later, many of these early pioneers have chosen to run guesthouses and countryside inns themselves, curating hotel stays that are a far cry from mass-produced, industrial tourism. Moving away from the masses to better protect their direct, natural environment and to cater to guests' needs, they positively impact each stay through knowledge, workshops, and discoveries. The new rurals favor the power of experience, with a focus on community and a desire to preserve tradition. From their gardens to their restaurants to their rooms, they are creating a richer tomorrow.

ABOVE   Forest cabins nestle among the evergreens at Nimmo Bay, Canada.

ABOVE   Deplar Farm, on the Troll Peninsula, Iceland, where the grass roofs change color with the seasons.

002 **In Praise of a New Form of Rurality**

008 THE ROOSTER
LIVADIA BAY—ANTIPAROS—GREECE

014 MASSERIA CALDERISI
FASANO—PUGLIA—ITALY

020 LE MOULIN
LOURMARIN—PROVENCE—FRANCE

026 DEXAMENES SEASIDE HOTEL
KOUROUTA—PELOPONNESE—GREECE

032 STORFJORD HOTEL AND OWNER'S CABIN
ÅLESUND—NORWAY

038 REFUGE DE LA TRAYE
LES ALLUES—SAVOIE—FRANCE

042 INNESS
ACCORD—NEW YORK—USA

048 **The Newt in Somerset**
A NEW VISION FOR THE ENGLISH COUNTRYSIDE

056 PARCO DEI SESI
PANTELLERIA—SICILY—ITALY

062 INIS MEÁIN RESTAURANT & SUITES
ARAN ISLANDS—COUNTY GALWAY—IRELAND

066 TOURISTS
NORTH ADAMS—MASSACHUSETTS—USA

072 ROSSO
ALLGÄU—BAVARIA—GERMANY

076 DOMAINE DE LA TRIGALIÈRE
AMBILLOU—TOURAINE—FRANCE

082 GRACE & SAVOUR, HAMPTON MANOR
HAMPTON IN ARDEN—WARWICKSHIRE—UK

088 HOTEL CRILLON LE BRAVE
VAUCLUSE—PROVENCE—FRANCE

092 MEZI PLŮTKY
ČELADNÁ—MORAVIA-SILESIA—CZECH REPUBLIC

096 ANSITZ HOHENEGG
GRÜNENBACH IM ALLGÄU—BAVARIA—GERMANY

102 **Unpacking the Power of Local Communities**

110 EBBIO
MONTERIGGIONI (SIENA)—TUSCANY—ITALY

116 L'ARMANCETTE
SAINT-NICOLAS DE VÉROCE—UVERGNE-RHÔNE-ALPES—FRANCE

120 BOVINA FARM & FERMENTORY
BOVINA—NEW YORK—USA

126 L'OVELLA NEGRA MOUNTAIN LODGE
INCLÊS VALLEY—ANDORRA

132 AUBERGE DE LA MAISON
COURMAYEUR—AOSTA VALLEY—ITALY

138 **Unearthing the Potential of the Land**

146 HECKFIELD PLACE
HECKFIELD—HAMPSHIRE—UK

152 DOMAINE LES BRUYÈRES
GAMBAIS—ÎLE-DE-FRANCE—FRANCE

158 DR. KAVVADIA'S ORGANIC FARM
TZAVROS—CORFU—GREECE

164 CASTELLO DI VICARELLO
CINIGIANO—TUSCANY—ITALY

170 **Finca La Donaira**
A NEW-AGE FINCA WHERE ALL THINGS GROW NATURALLY

178 QUINTA DA CÔRTE
TABUAÇO—DOURO—PORTUGAL

184 MALHADINHA NOVA
ALBERNOA—ALENTEJO—PORTUGAL

188 METOHI KINDELIS
CHANIA—CRETE—GREECE

192 **Rural Traditions, the New Way Forward**

200 VILLA LENA
PALAIA—TUSCANY—ITALY

206 CASA BALANDRA
PÒRTOL—MALLORCA—SPAIN

212 KRANICH MUSEUM & HOTEL
HESSENBURG / SAAL—MECKLENBURG-WESTERN POMERANIA—GERMANY

218 VIPP FARMHOUSE
SØLLESTED—LOLLAND—DENMARK

222 ALMIÈRES
LOZÈRE—OCCITANIE—FRANCE

228 EREMITO
PARRANO—UMBRIA—ITALY

232 **A Sense of Place in Rural Areas**

240 ADEGA DO FOGO
PICO ISLAND—AZORES—PORTUGAL

246 EUMELIA
LACONIA—PELOPONNESE—GREECE

250 CAPTAINS REST
STRAHAN—TASMANIA—AUSTRALIA

256 **Șesuri**
A PROJECT COMMITTED TO SUSTAINABILITY AND LOCAL TRADITIONS IN ROMANIA

264 GUARDSWELL FARM
PERTHSHIRE—SCOTLAND—UK

270 DEPLAR FARM
FLJÓT VALLEY—TROLL PENINSULA—ICELAND

276 FOGO ISLAND INN
JOE BATT'S ARM—NEWFOUNDLAND—CANADA

282 ILIMANAQ LODGE
DISKO BAY—QAASUITSUP MUNICIPALITY—GREENLAND

286 INDEX

The Rooster

Respect for Greek Traditions Defines The Rooster

LIVADIA BAY
|
ANTIPAROS
|
GREECE

Set above a wild beach and a protected creek on the Greek island of Antiparos, the 16 villas of The Rooster retreat and slow farm blend in with the Mediterranean landscape. Working with Vois Architects and local artisans and makers, daughter of a Greek shipowner Athanasia Comninos has created a contemporary yet timeless resort where the very principles of Cycladic architecture are at play: low-rise villas with dry-stone walls create intimacy, while large openings engage visitors in dialogue with the sea.

"From the start, my aim for The Rooster was to protect nature," explains Athanasia. "The surrounding landscape and beauty of this wonderful island. I wanted to turn back the hands of time, so I followed that vision. Traditional and local building techniques use plaster, stone, terra-cotta, wood, and iron, so that is what we resorted to in building The Rooster in the most sustainable way."

Timeless designs, black-and-white photography, vintage furniture, natural fabrics, and elegantly rough wall finishes give a wabi-sabi touch to the interiors. It feels natural to see no trace of plastic throughout The Rooster and all the way to the farm where vegetables, herbs, and seasonal fruits are grown. Drinking water can be scarce on the island, so a borehole was drilled, and the water is now cleaned and purified using a biological system. Together with a chicken coop and a kitchen team that uses leftovers and vegetable waste to create natural compost, the farm is setting the mark for locals and visitors to act and eat responsibly.

The same goes for the beach in front of The Rooster: guests find no umbrellas or lounge chairs here. "I have

OPPOSITE   Built using soft yellow stone and reeded canopies, The Rooster's 16 villas have been designed to blend seamlessly with the rugged local terrain.

ABOVE AND OPPOSITE (TOP)   Rainforest showers and private pools allow guests to bathe and relax in the open, surrounded by the sounds and scents of their natural surroundings.

ABOVE   Delicious meals at The Rooster use ingredients sourced from local farmers and fishermen, as well as rich pickings from the fruits and vegetables grown on its own farm.

ANTIPAROS
GREECE

012

ABOVE AND OPPOSITE (TOP) Oases of calm, The Rooster's villas have romantic names, depending on their location, including Wilderness Valley, Bush & Hill, and Haven of Tranquility.

been going to this beach for ten years," says Athanasia. "No one owns beaches in Greece, although some act as if they do. Why would I invade such a wonderful beach with furniture? I have countless childhood memories of us carrying picnic baskets along and having fresh fruits. I decided to go back in time and bring them back."

In the main kitchen, chef Andreas Nikolakopoulos sources a creative menu from local ingredients: marinated caper leaves, a collection of olive varieties, olive oil infused with the resort's own rosemary, vegetables freshly picked from the garden, and seafood delivered by local fishermen. Here, the Greek way of life takes center stage with 21st-century sophistication. Overlooking the unspoiled creek, modernity seems to have found its pace. As Athanasia says, "keeping the landscape as it is was our number one rule."

ABOVE Delicious meals at The Rooster use ingredients sourced from local farmers and fishermen, as well as rich pickings from the fruits and vegetables grown on its own farm.

Masseria Calderisi

A Puglian Masseria Where Traditions Are Alive and Renewed

FASANO
|
PUGLIA
|
ITALY

Minutes from the Adriatic Coast, the intimate family-owned boutique hotel, Masseria Calderisi, stands within 8 hectares (20 acres) of secluded olive and citrus groves, almond trees, herb gardens, and vegetable beds in the Puglian countryside. Blending contemporary design with farm-to-fork dining, German couple Max and Jutta von Braunmühl have brought life back to the traditional 17th-century farmhouse.

"Much of the ancient Masseria was constructed from tufa stone, quarried from the grounds of the property itself," explains the couple. "While renovating it, we intervened seamlessly to keep the original structures, traditionally built-in whitewashed stone, as well as historic details such as high vaulted ceilings, stone fireplaces, and alcoves embedded in the deep walls."

In addition, they converted an original block of stables into five suites, flanked by private patios and olive trees; the secluded Il Fortino suite lies beside a private walled garden and pool, concealed among the estate's ancient olive groves. Respectful of the rural surroundings, the interiors—designed by Jutta together with a team of creatives and artisans—combine local materials with international touches. Sofas and armchairs clad in white French linen team up with wicker baskets, woven lamps, and oak coffee tables, while bronze handles created by a foundry in Brescia decorate the doors and cabinetry. In the bathrooms, blue, yellow, and orange tiles alternate to recall the colors of the Adriatic Coast, while ceramic objects from the nearby city of Grottaglie, including sculptures and plates by artist Enza Fasano, hint at local traditions.

OPPOSITE   Narrow pathways flanked by low stone walls wind their way through the estate, linking accommodations to the farmhouse, its terraces, and the olive groves beyond.

PUGLIA
ITALY

TOP LEFT   The stable suites have front and rear outdoor spaces. Sitting out front, guests look out toward the farmhouse.

ABOVE (BOTTOM)   A historic tower has been renovated to contain two suites. Beneath vaulted stone ceilings, each suite has a living room, separate bedroom, and en suite shower.

ABOVE Toward the rear, a walled garden offers privacy.

ABOVE Max and Jutta have done much to retain original features of the 17th-century farmhouse, such as this wonderful, soft stone doorway, with neoclassical pediment and fluting.

Equally eager to uphold regional customs, chef Pietro Sgaramella bakes his own bread, cakes, and focaccia in the centuries-old stone oven, along with freshly fired pizzas. Often referred to as "the farm of Italy," Puglia has a strong agricultural heritage and is celebrated for its fresh produce: at Masseria Calderisi's restaurant La Corte, guests dine on organic produce grown in the hotel's gardens and groves, as well as mozzarella and organic beef sourced from nearby farms and fish and seafood supplied by local fishermen. After a meal, guests can head to the Calderisi beach a stone's throw away, turning Masseria Calderisi into a truly self-sufficient destination.

ABOVE   There is much emphasis on being out of doors, whether spending time at the beach, on the farm, or enjoying candlelit downtime with fellow guests at the aperitivo terrace bar.

Le Moulin

A Historic Hotel Brings Back Local Village Life

LOURMARIN | PROVENCE | FRANCE

At the heart of Lourmarin, a picturesque village in Provence, Le Moulin is named after an old oil mill—the 18th-century wheel is still visible at the center of the main restaurant. It would have been easy to imagine a hotel catering for wealthy Americans with a passion for Provence, but Eric Dardé's approach was quite the opposite: the self-made hotelier and president of the small hotel group Beaumier likes giving and pleasing. "I started as a waiter, and for me, it all still comes down to sharing essential moments and bringing softness and tenderness to a place," he explains. "I wanted to put Le Moulin back at the center of the village, involve and welcome local villagers without false intentions or promises."

Le Moulin is a good example of how to reconnect with a village's rich local heritage. It is less about creating new experiences than reenacting the past. The hotel lobby takes shape as a convivial bar, where guests meet with the locals as they check in. The outdoor terrace is more like a central plaza where locals and tourists form a seamless crowd as they order a *pastis* beneath a jute awning. Open to all, the adjacent gourmet *épicerie* sells the best regional produce as well as pastries. Close to the kitchen back door, it is stocked with the freshest items and conjures the very notion of village life. For those in need of shade and discretion, an interior garden is organized like a green protected patio.

The interiors, designed by rising French architectural duo Jaune and creatives at studio be-poles, feature local hues, artisanal furnishings, and the rustic vibe of rural Provence. During renovation,

OPPOSITE The center of village life, Le Moulin is the epitome of conviviality, with a host of welcoming indoor and outdoor spaces to stop for a chat over coffee or a bite to eat.

PROVENCE
FRANCE

022

ABOVE AND OPPOSITE (TOP)   Generous rooms are decorated simply with sisal walls and floors, woven rush furnishings, and terra-cotta wares—all in muted Provencal colors.

LE MOULIN

a stone foyer staircase with wrought-metal detailing was kept, while lime plaster was applied on the walls to lighten the place up. Dried local flowers are displayed on the tables and beautiful, handcrafted earthenware includes glazed tiles made in Millau by Terres Cuites de Raujolles. The palette of pale shades, sisal yellow, and ocher red is inspired by colors found in the earth locally—Luberon's ocher deposits were once quarried extensively.

"We try to craft environments that make sense. For us, well-being naturally comes through sourcing natural, local goodness, whether people, objects, or fresh produce," explains Eric. "What if modern-day hoteliers thought of their operations like a village plaza where one stops for coffee, initiates a conversation with a neighbor, reads, sunbathes, and dreams?"

ABOVE   Dining at Le Moulin can be a simple affair, with meals focused on regional dishes made with fresh, locally sourced ingredients—salads, savory tarts, and terrines.

PROVENCE
FRANCE

ABOVE Guests staying at the hotel have the choice of eating inside the restaurant or in the garden—a popular spot in summer, shaded by canopies.

ABOVE   The hub of the hotel is the large, open foyer with floor-to-ceiling windows and solid, rough-hewn stone walls set against walls plastered in lime.

Dexamenes Seaside Hotel

The Industrial Transformed into a Sustainable Design Hotel

KOUROUTA | PELOPONNESE | GREECE

Once a wine factory set directly on the Ionian Sea in the Peloponnese, today Dexamenes is Greece's most-singular postindustrial hotel. An architectural slice of Greek trading history, the 1920s steel and concrete tanks take visitors back to a time when the Greeks established wineries and distilleries to export wine. The Karaflos family purchased the abandoned site in 2003, with ambitions of turning it into a hotel. Completing his studies as an engineer at the time, Nikos Karaflos had no desire to get involved with the project, but the idea grew on him: "There was no life in the property, yet there was a strong feeling," he explains. "The challenge was to bring new life into it, to connect the building with modern times."

Briefing architects K-Studio in 2010, Nikos wanted to keep the site as natural as possible; instinctively, his plan was to make it sustainable and to minimize waste. As a result, concrete blocks carved out to create doorways have been used as stepping-stones for the pool, the handrails on the promenade are composed of upcycled water pipes, and all the floors use bricks reclaimed from the walls of the warehouse. Nikos knew all contractors and suppliers, so the project was driven naturally by local talents.

Guests are invited to live locally, through ethically sourced local food, regional recipes, and biodynamic wines. Acclaimed chef Gikas Xenakis (from Aleria, Athens) created the menu with sustainability and seasonality at heart: his team is in constant dialogue with local producers, who come to the resort bringing samples and freshly harvested goodness. Guests can also visit producers and harvest in season. "We want

OPPOSITE   The Dexamenes Seaside Hotel has direct access to the golden sands of Kourouta Beach on the west coast of the Peloponnese.

PELOPONNESE
GREECE

028

ABOVE   Accommodations at the hotel are set within the former winery's 34 wine tanks and are categorized as "beachfront" (top), "courtyard" (bottom), and "backyard" (opposite).

guests to learn about nature and where their food comes from," explains Nikos. "Today, urban and rural life are at odds. For our mental and physical health, we need to stitch them back together and reconnect to nature. We need to build urban resilience, be as local as possible, and go back to the roots of rural culture."

Through many events, which locals also attend, Dexamenes Seaside Hotel has established itself as an open creative platform. Events include sound performances and light installations inside the silo, readings based on the Greek landscape, workshops on seeds in the Mediterranean garden, and talks with architects. Dexamenes seems to have it all covered.

ABOVE   All of the rooms are designed with the same postindustrial aesthetic using steel, glass, and timber, giving new life to the original structures here.

PELOPONNESE
GREECE

ABOVE All of the suites have their own patios. Toward the rear of the development, overlooking the hotel's vineyard, the backyard wine tank suites are quiet and secluded.

Storfjord Hotel and Owner's Cabin

Sustainability Drives Experiential Travel with 62°NORD

Storfjord Hotel is a small, timber, luxury hotel overlooking the Storfjord and Sunnmore Alps on the western coast of Norway. Nestled in the woods, it takes shape as a cluster of Norwegian cabins and wooden houses with 30 rooms for guests scattered among them. Preserving tradition and creating a mountain-lodge feel, the roofs of the cabins are covered in green grass and moss.

This forest hotel is one of several properties owned and run by Ålesund-based experiential travel company 62°NORD, founded by Knut Flakk, who also runs a wool-based garment-making business, among others. At the heart of both ventures are a love of farming (Knut was raised on a farm), the great outdoors, the power of nature, and tradition. "Some choices are more important than others. Don't buy or consume more than you need: choose natural and choose what will last for generations," says Knut.

ÅLESUND
|
NORWAY

Storfjord Hotel nurtures longstanding relationships with the nearby village of Glomset and small businesses and local communities to source artisanal produce, to host baking classes, and to organize fishing trips with a local captain and hikes with an expert local guide. The conscious woodland retreat also runs a restaurant called The Kitchen, which thrives on local produce.

Also among 62°NORD properties is Owner's Cabin, a small cottage set on the secluded island of Giske that has been reimagined as a self-catering retreat. Uniquely Norwegian in the way it is secluded yet reliably comfortable, Owner's Cabin is furnished with old linens, rural artifacts, and countless books. Surrounded by untouched land, it has direct access to small beaches and the North Sea—home to colonies of seals and passing orcas.

OPPOSITE An outdoor living room at the Storfjord Hotel. In the Scandinavian spirit of *friluftsliv*, spending time outside is good for the soul, no matter what the weather.

ÅLESUND
NORWAY

Both properties have a sense of place, they employ local staff, source regional products, and invite guests to slow down. Kurt runs 62°NORD like his other businesses—that is, according to the triple-bottom-line theory: planet, people, and profit, in that order. As Kurt says himself: "There is a growing awareness for the need to protect nature, and as a businessman, I can contribute. My aim is to provide hospitality the Norwegian way, preserving culture, empowering people, and protecting nature."

ABOVE   In the monochromatic winter landscape, the hotel cabins blend in with their surroundings, their grassy roofs a rusty orange in harmony with the garden vegetation.

ABOVE Inside the hotel, rooms with dark, paneled walls and comfortable armchairs set the scene for a cozy night after a long hike in the open country.

STORFJORD HOTEL AND OWNER'S CABIN

ÅLESUND
NORWAY

036

ABOVE   The view across Storfjord from the wooded
hillside on which the hotel stands. Rising above the water
are the Sunnmøre Alps.

STORFJORD HOTEL
AND OWNER'S CABIN

037

Refuge de la Traye

A Renovated Alpine Hamlet That Takes Travelers Back in Time

LES ALLUES
|
SAVOIE
|
FRANCE

Set in a remote landscape above the village of Les Allues in the Méribel ski resort, Refuge de la Traye's 12 chalets stand surrounded by the pristine wilderness of the French Alps. Designed to look and feel like a traditional Savoie hamlet, the chalets vary in size and function to provide a hotel with six rooms and all of the luxury services guests could possibly need.

In winter, experienced skiers can access the hamlet by backcountry skiing, while others can use an electric snowcat that meanders up the steep forest paths. At the entrance to the resort, the small Saint-Bernard's Chapel dedicated to the patron of the Alps and mountaineers stands the test of time. Beyond, with a nod to vernacular traditions, but also sustainability, the chalets have been built using natural materials typical of the region—old larch wood and stone from the surrounding mountains. Members of Les Compagnons du Devoir, an organization of French craftsmen and artisans dating back to the Middle Ages, were enlisted for their expertise in "building according to centuries-old traditions."

Inside, the refuge the decor follows a classic Alpine code: old wildlife paintings, sculpted wooden furnishings, low-beamed ceilings, cowbells, traditional textiles and rugs made from Savoie sheep wool, and stag-horn chandeliers. Collectible plates line the walls of the restaurant, in which traditional regional dishes are served, including crozets (local, square buckwheat pasta) prepared with Beaufort cheese and, sometimes, foraged mushrooms. Additional Alpine treats include whiling away the hours in front of the fireplace, sampling local wines, jams, and cheese as well as honey from the refuge's beehives, and enjoying

OPPOSITE Looking toward the stone Saint-Bernard's Chapel at the entrance to the hamlet. In the foreground are two of the site's smaller chalets.

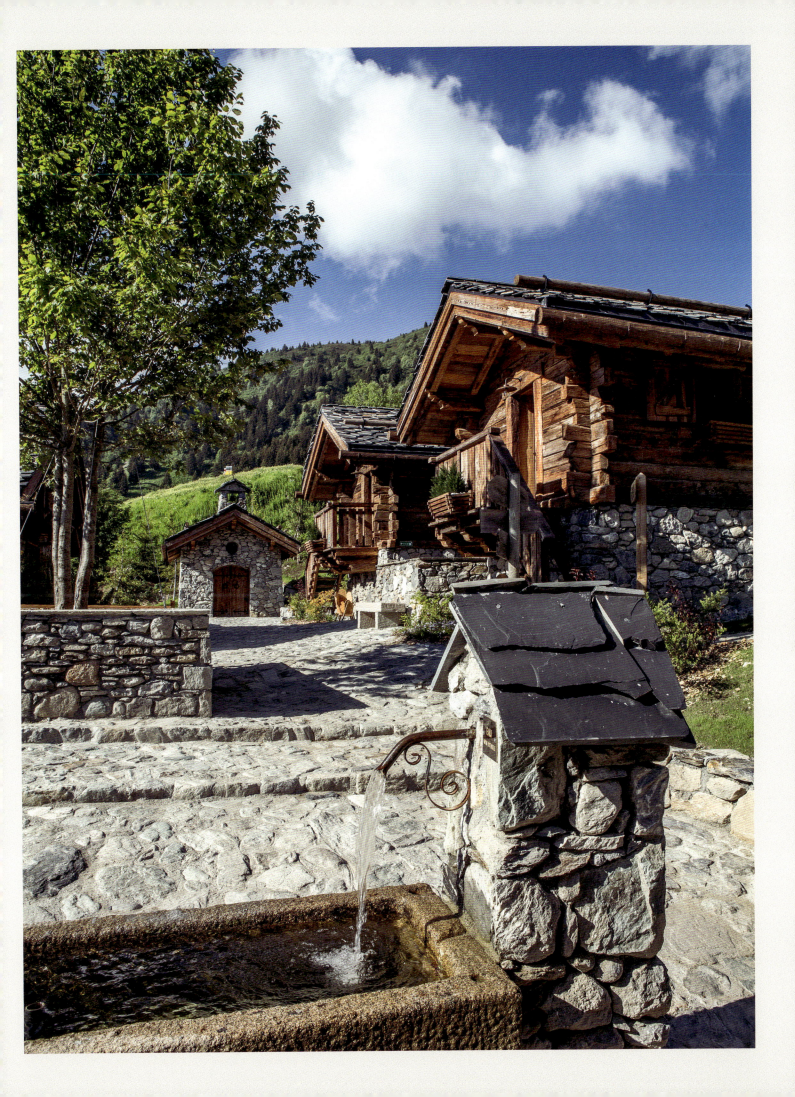

SAVOIE
FRANCE

040

ABOVE   Each of the suites and rooms in the hotel is named for an Alpine flower and decorated in colors that reflect the meadows in spring. This is the Orchidée suite.

REFUGE DE LA TRAYE

organic seasonal produce sourced from local farms. "In the mountains, a refuge is a safe place, somewhere to shelter during a snowstorm. Refuge de la Traye was designed as an escape from everyday life, a place to reconnect with both oneself and nature," explains managing director Gilles Lenzlinger. In embracing the true roots of a mountain retreat, Refuge de la Traye does exactly that.

TOP   The stunningly fresh Alpine countryside.

BOTTOM   The hotel offers a host of luxury spa treatments including milk baths (pictured) and hay beds.

INNESS

A Respite from Urban Living with a New Kind of Rural Cabin Stay

ACCORD | NEW YORK | USA

The 40-room countryside refuge and members club INNESS sits on 90 hectares (225 acres) of pastoral land in the Catskills, just a 90-minute drive from New York City. Of the hotel's rooms, 28 exist as cabins within the grounds. The remaining 12 rooms occupy space in the Farmhouse, which is also home to a restaurant and lounge. Additional features, besides numerous hiking trails, include an events barn, the Farm Shop, and a 1.2-hectare (3-acre) organic farm—all imagined by landscape designer Miranda Brooks using indigenous flora.

Responding to the property's ethos—"the juxtaposition of the cultivated and the wild"—INNESS is named after the prominent American landscape painter George Inness. In tribute to the artist, the retreat was conceived by a group of designers and developers, who regularly escape the city to reconnect with the Hudson Valley's bountiful nature. The result is a collection of minimal vernacular buildings designed to blend in with the bucolic landscape. Drawing inspiration from New England's colonial architecture, for example, New York designer Taavo Somer teamed up with Post Company to create cabins with a residential feel.

At the center of the property, the organic farm and orchard not only supplies the restaurant but also engages members of the surrounding community through education and events. The restaurant's menu thrives on local produce and further highlights seasonal offerings from the Hudson Valley, including dishes prepared al fresco on the property's outdoor smokers and grills. Beyond providing nourishing food for the local and greater community, the mission of the farm is to offer meaningful hands-on

OPPOSITE The retreat's "cultivated wild" ethos is beautifully encapsulated in Miranda Brooks' landscaping, which balances untamed growth with areas of formality.

NEW YORK
USA

ABOVE AND OPPOSITE (TOP)   The interior design at INNESS is carefully curated with the intention of recalling the artisan craftsmanship of the region.

ABOVE The estate sits in the most bucolic surroundings; the desire at INNESS is to evoke an earlier, less complicated time, surrounded by nature.

NEW YORK
USA

046

ABOVE   The house has been designed and the cabins
positioned so that most rooms have captivating views of nature.

education for all ages and to build bonds through food and farming.

Year-round, seasonal produce, coffee, and home-baked goods are available for purchase at the Farm Shop, which looks like a simple greenhouse. Inside the light-filled structure lies an oasis of curated wares and home essentials, from locally made ceramics to clothing. With the intention of taking the farm-shop concept further, the expansive space is fitted out with movable metal seating, so that guests can pull up a chair and congregate with coffee, surrounded by greenery and children. Hosting a program of communal events, the venue seeks to reimagine the idea of the rural village center.

TOP INNESS prides itself on providing seasonal dishes made with locally sourced and homegrown ingredients. The menu is primarily Mediterranean inspired.

BRUTON   SOMERSET   UK

A New Vision for the English Countryside

THE NEWT IN
SOMERSET

The Newt in Somerset is a luxury hospitality project that combines legendary gardens, farms, orchards, and vegetable plots with a Georgian country house and a historic farm hamlet.

Set in the southwest of England, the beauty of The Newt in Somerset's flowered gardens, apple orchards, centennial trees, old stones and farmsteads is impossible to deny. Elevated from the past and brought back to life, the estate is as unconventional as its owner and creative eye, South African Karen Roos. "I have always been committed to fighting conservatisms," she says, "I don't want to please nor be loved through my projects, I want them to be an open-minded, forward-thinking expression of our times." That was already true of Karen and her husband Koos Bekker's first project, Babylonstoren, an old farm outside Cape Town, South Africa. The once declining 1,200-hectare (3,000-acre) estate is now lush with vineyards, olive and citrus groves, endless rows of fruit trees, walled vegetable gardens, and hills covered in prickly pear cactuses and rooibos tea bushes. Countless gardeners rush around the place, a veritable hive of activity. "I felt my husband needed to reconnect with the land," Karen recalls. "At first, he saw in Babylonstoren a place to escape on weekends. I should have been more suspicious!"

After turning Babylonstoren into a successful, world-class operating farm and lifestyle destination, the couple found their next project an hour outside of London in Somerset. "When we first visited Hadspen House in 2014, we realized it was built in 1790, a few years apart from Babylonstoren," Karen notes, "like the latter, there was little left of the 325-hectare (800-acre) estate's past grandeur and garden." Having purchased the house and its land, Karen and Koos enlisted the help of friend and landscaper Patrice Taravella to carry out the extensive renovation. It took two years to recreate the historical gardens, to plant orchards and vegetable gardens.

Today, the botanical gardens are open to the public and include a cider house and press, where daily visits and tastings occur; a bakery, ice cream, and farm shop that sells homegrown and homemade products; a Victorian greenhouse that serves as a teahouse and space for workshops; and an apiary called the Beezantium. Designed by Invisible Studio in collaboration with beekeeper Paula Carnell, the Beezantium is an apiary that includes habitats for wild bees, solitary bees, and wild swarms that need to be relocated or moved when trees fall.

No less work was put into the historic houses, accommodations, and restaurants. Karen spent two years at Hadspen House composing what she equates to a real-life film set, imagining who lived there "and how I could translate it today with a modern twist," she explains. Colorful and sustainable Ames furniture sits in the winter garden, modern lime-green ceramic counters enliven the bar in the restaurant, old paintings and contemporary photographs mix and match, and antique wooden paneling creates warmth inside the Botanical Rooms bistronomic restaurant.

"I always wanted to engage with projects that unite local talents and invite them to participate," explains Karen. "I believe in people, artists, and artisans to create inspiring, beautiful, useful, and accessible content. That belief helped me a lot when I started in the hospitality industry." The latest addition to the property does just that. Set in a valley beyond the cider orchard, and with an additional 17-rooms, the Farmyard complements the existing 23-room Georgian manor perfectly. Housed in a former dairy, the design pays tribute to the property's original 18th-century farmhouse buildings: the barns, stable, granary, and cider press. While respecting the architectural legacy of the buildings, architect Richard Parr worked in close collaboration with Karen to modernize them using local materials: stone from a nearby quarry, Cornish slate, forest marble, oak, and glass.

Back on the land and the working farm, a passionate team of farmers, gardeners, butchers, bakers, cheesemakers, chefs, and cider makers work in harmony with the seasons, the land, and livestock. As such, The Newt in Somerset follows the example set by Babylonstoren, where more than 300 varieties of edible or medicinal plants grow—all plants on the property are grown as organically as possible and in a biologically sustainable manner. Harvested daily, The Newt's gardens produce fruits and vegetables used in the two farm-to-fork restaurants. Head chef of the Botanical Rooms restaurant, award-winning Ben Champkin, composes a daily feast from estate-grown vegetables, the choicest cuts from the salt room, and dayboat fish from the Dorset coast. Responding to a growing demand, boxes of fresh fruits and vegetables are also delivered weekly to conscious food lovers.

"The estate has grown so much," says Karen. "The key is to pull talent together and keep an eye on everything all the time for it to have a personality of its own in the end. Being singular takes a lot of work; it gets you out of your comfort zone. You have to be ready for what is coming next and choose carefully."

THE NEWT IN SOMERSET

051

TOP   The Newt's handsome Georgian limestone house is surrounded by farmland, orchards, lakes, and woodland.

BOTTOM   The bright and colorful croquet lounge.

SOMERSET
UK

TOP   The Garden View Room in Hadspen House. All of the rooms at The Newt are exquisitely decorated, primarily with a muted palette and occasional pops of color.

ABOVE AND OPPOSITE (BOTTOM) The estate's kitchen garden and orchards supply the hotel's restaurants and café with fresh, seasonal fruits, herbs, and vegetables year-round.

SOMERSET
UK

054

ABOVE   On the grounds of The Newt, "The Story of Gardening" exhibition explores the concept of the garden through time and the impact it has had on culture.

ABOVE   On and around the estate, farmers, gardeners, butchers, and cheesemakers work in harmony with the land to produce food for the table.

Parco dei Sesi

In Praise of a Centuries-Old Natural Way of Living

PANTELLERIA
|
SICILY
|
ITALY

A timeless property in the heart of the Sesi Archaeological Park on the island of Pantelleria, Parco dei Sesi is an organic farm set within a megalithic stone village. The architecture blends in seamlessly with its surroundings and 13 luxury rooms set within original *dammuso* houses invite guests to live the slow life in the most natural of environments.

This magical island between Sicily and Tunisia is quite unlike any other Mediterranean destination, with its unique landscape of black volcanic stones and rocky beaches, palm trees, and bougainvillea. It was a fascination for this rugged, arid, ancient corner of the world that inspired Parisian Margot Guelfi and Milanese-Sicilian Massimiliano Panseca to swap their busy city lives for a more rural one, with the establishment of their farm. The property features numerous *muri a secchi* (drystone walls) that date back 5,000 years. Equally old are the megalithic thumbs, known as sese, that dot the landscape—remnants of the island's first civilization. Margot and Massimiliano took great care to restore the abandoned parts of the park around the house. They preserved the ancient buildings, renovating the dome roofs that channel rainwater into underground cisterns. Inside the dammuso houses, they created stripped-down, elegant interiors whose thick black stone walls are covered in bare plaster. Built-in stone benches and bed platforms are complemented by vintage furniture bought in French flea markets and woven lampshades.

In Pantelleria, conditions are so harsh that, even today, the fields are worked by hand. Margot and Massimiliano have learned a lot from the local farmers,

OPPOSITE   A stone arch marks the entrance to the Parco dei Sesi retreat, flanked by lush beds of vegetation, lovingly restored by Margot Guelfi and Massimiliano Panseca.

SICILY
ITALY

058

ABOVE   Parco dei Sesi offers guests the opportunity to explore the rugged volcanic landscape of the archaeological park in which the retreat is situated.

ABOVE At the main house, a shady veranda is set for lunch. Menus change daily, based on locally sourced and homegrown ingredients.

ABOVE   Il Grande Dammuso is a self-contained, self-catered guesthouse, with accommodations for a large group and its own private outdoor spaces.

PARCO DEI SESI

whose knowledge has been passed down through the generations: crops of capers, olives, and vines are pruned extremely low to protect their fruits and guarantee a small yield of exquisite quality. Chickens scratch around the grounds, and the goats that provide fresh milk roam around the property. Come lunchtime, a zero-mile feast of local wine, tomatoes from the garden, sardines, capers, and rye bread is put together simply. Later, a dinner cooked entirely from local produce is served. Nothing seems to have changed for centuries. Margot sums it up perfectly: "Time stopped running here a while ago."

ABOVE   All of the rooms and suites at Parco dei Sesi are decorated similarly, with plastered walls and textiles in a range of soft, neutral tones.

Inis Meáin Restaurant & Suites

A Tasteful Remote Refuge on a Secluded Island

ARAN ISLANDS
|
COUNTY GALWAY
|
IRELAND

Inis Meáin is one of the smallest islands of the Aran Archipelago located 20 kilometers (12,4 miles) off the west coast of Ireland. At just 5 kilometers long and 3 kilometers wide (3×2 miles), this tiny islet looks like a raw limestone slab in the wild Atlantic Ocean. Home to around 150 living souls, it is also the site of the Inis Meáin Restaurant & Suites, a five-suite luxury nature lodge with a renowned seasonal restaurant, run by Marie-Thérèse and her husband, accomplished chef Ruairí de Blacam.

Famous for their breathtaking landscape, beautiful coastal scenery, wild flora and fauna, archaeological sites, and authentic Irish culture, the Aran Islands are somewhat lost in time.

Although the retreat is contemporary in its design, Irish architecture firm de Blacam & Meagher took inspiration from the landscape to help it blend in with its surroundings. With facades of local, hand-carved limestone, the exteriors melt into the island terrain while large bay windows offer endless panoramic views, in both the restaurant and suites.

Perfectly in tune with the elements, Inis Meáin's restaurant is a destination in itself. Acclaimed, it uses ingredients harvested on or around the island: lobster and crab are caught by local fishermen from currachs, the traditional island fishing boats, and vegetables, fruits, and herbs are grown by the de Blacams using island seaweed as fertilizer. When the season permits, foraging is a daily habit. A keen baker and gardener, Marie-Thérèse crafts breads, cakes, and cookies daily and oversees the gardens. Here, equal attention is given to the tomatoes as they grow in the greenhouse

OPPOSITE   At dusk, the warm glow of the setting sun is reflected in the panoramic ribbon of windows that encircles the building.

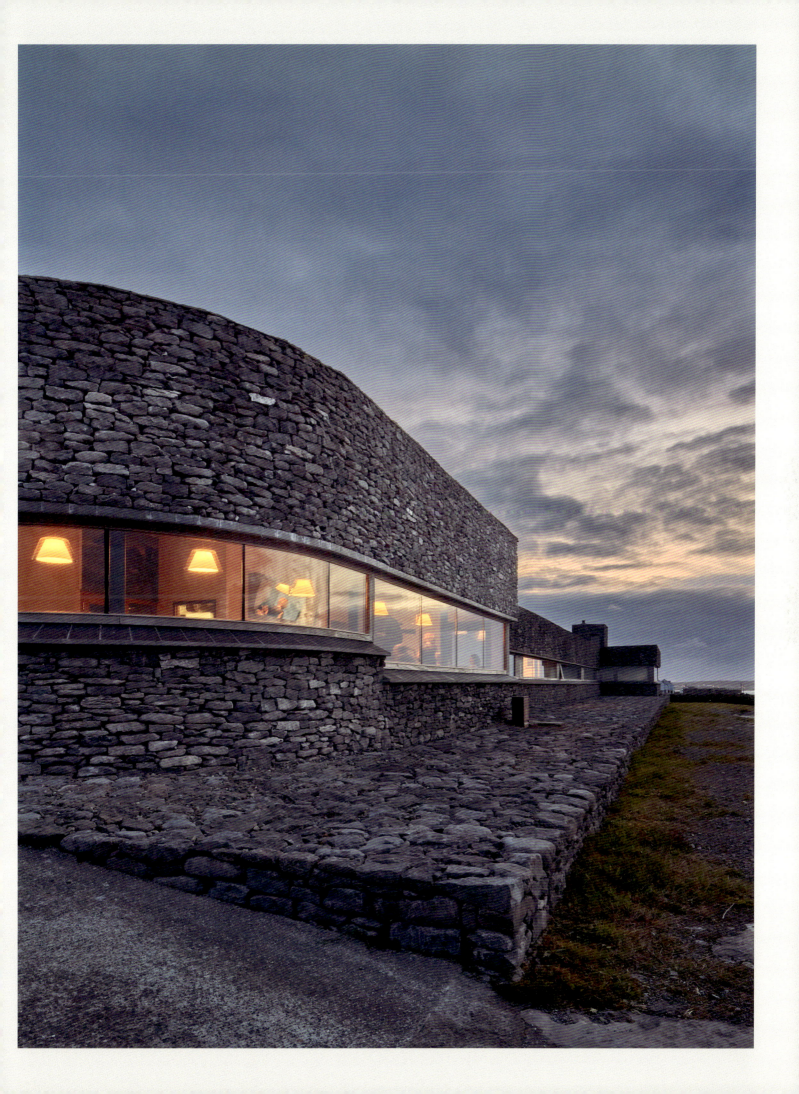

COUNTY GALWAY
IRELAND

TOP LEFT AND ABOVE In each of the five suites at Inis Meáin, an expanse of glass reveals panoramic views of the island and sea; furnishings focus on natural materials.

TOP RIGHT A sea urchin picked fresh from the sea.

outside the restaurant, the bread warm from the oven, or the lobster chosen from the island pier.

A cultural stronghold, Inis Meáin Restaurant & Suites defends timeless values and local traditions both inside and outside the retreat. Restful, the suites' expansive views are complemented by interiors crafted using local materials, such as wood, lime, stone, and wool. Outside, guests are encouraged to explore the island's rugged natural terrain and old ruins on bicycle or foot and to stop by the internationally renowned Inis Meáin Knitting Company factory store before socializing in the traditional island pub.

TOP   Looking across the island of Inis Meáin, the countryside crisscrossed with numerous drystone walls. Easily traversed on foot, it is a haven for hikers.

TOURISTS

An American Classic Remodeled for the 21st-Century Traveler

NORTH ADAMS
|
MASSACHUSETTS
|
USA

Set on the banks of the Hoosic River in North Adams, Massachusetts, TOURISTS is a hotel and riverside retreat inspired by the classic American roadside motor lodge. Designed for the 21st-century traveler, the 48-room property is a clever union of never-too-serious elevated design, creativity, and nature. Take the hotel's name, for example, which was inspired by a "Tourists Welcome" sign that once graced the property. Set on 20 hectares (50 acres) of land that surround the Hoosic River, TOURISTS is blessed with woodland trails, riverbank vistas, and sculptural installations—a reminder that the Massachusetts Museum of Contemporary Art, which revived the formerly industrial town of North Adams, is only a few minutes' drive away.

At the helm of the TOURISTS vision is a team of independent creatives: Ben Svenson is the hotel's lead partner and designer. Working alongside him are John Stirratt, bassist and founder of indie rock band Wilco; Eric Kerns, cofounder of Bright Ideas brewery; Scott Stedman, head of *Brooklyn Magazine*; and Corey Wentworth, formerly of Boston's Flour Bakery. But it was architect Henry Scollard (founder of HANK) and "creator of spaces" Julie Pearson (of Spartan Shop) who were responsible for giving the '60s motor lodge inn its new lease on life as a hip country hotel. Expertly, they created an alluring destination: TOURISTS simply strikes a balance between summer-camp conviviality and the quiet you expect of a proper rural retreat. Imagine carefully curated interiors composed of hand-picked vintage furniture, rural objects, minimalist plywood beds, and contemporary art, all housed in a 1960s ranch home. The picture-perfect

OPPOSITE   A cozy log fire burns on the communal deck. Beyond, the cabins snake around a large, beautifully planted garden that sits at the heart of the development.

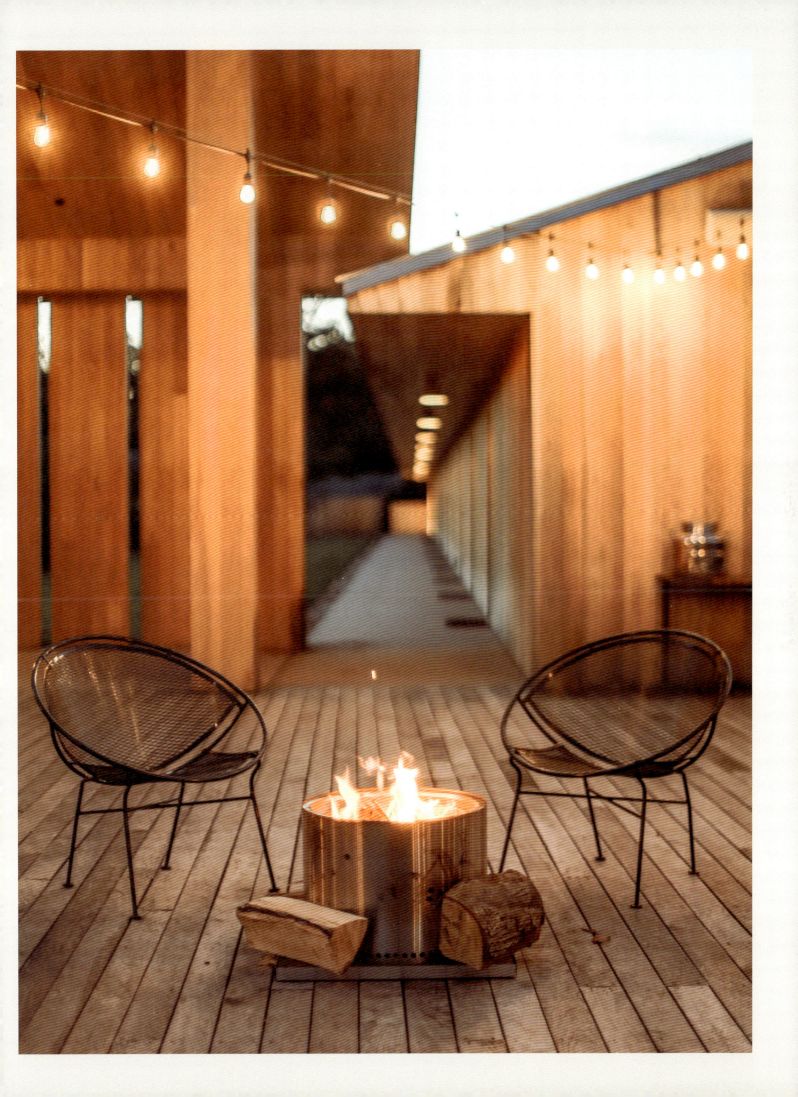

MASSACHUSETTS
USA

068

ABOVE   This is just a small corner of the vast, communal lodge space, a timber-lined room furnished with mid-century classics arranged around an impressive fireplace.

lobby features a rare find: vintage tan Mario Bellini Camaleonda sofas.

Drawing on a network of local talents, artisans, and producers, the hotel's restaurant was first established by celebrated chef Cortney Burns. Prior to the opening, Cortney worked with the North Adams Historical Society, and found old community cookbooks that had the imprint of many cultures all over them: "Irish, French Canadian, Italian, Welsh, Lebanese, Jewish, and Chinese immigrants all left their mark on North Adams," she recalls. These helped her shape her vision for the restaurant, which quite literally brings together cultures, recipes, and people. "What if the Italians asked to borrow sugar from the neighbor next door, and they got rosewater instead?" she asks. "The restaurant is a gathering place where culture is shared, people break bread, and share time."

TOP   A table set for dinner at The Airport Rooms restaurant. The decor here has a distinctly retro vibe and sets a convivial tone for communal eating.

MASSACHUSETTS
USA

070

ABOVE   Each cabin has large windows and decking to the rear, placing guests meters from the stunning woodland and river landscape that surrounds the site.

ABOVE   A large, decked communal space sits at one end of the development—the perfect chill-out zone for gazing at Massachusetts' night skies.

Rosso

A Wooden Farm That Feels Like Home

ALLGÄU
|
BAVARIA
|
GERMANY

Nested close to the Alps, between Munich and Lake Constance in southern Germany, Rosso is an old farmstead that stands out among the meadows, hills, and cow-filled pastures. With three luxury-style, self-contained apartments, the original farm has been reimagined by owners Christian Müller and Lisa Rühwald and transformed into a countryside retreat. To them, it serves as an idyllic basecamp from which to start a journey; a haven to rest in; and a place for old and new friends, nearby guests, or faraway visitors. "Rosso is yours to make," they say.

Behind the wooden facade of the old farmhouse, and beneath its original beams, Rosso's three apartments share an eclectic mix of traditional Bavarian furniture, vintage pieces and flea-market curiosities, Mediterranean-inspired tadelakt-plastered bathrooms, and wabi-sabi objects. Each has a large kitchen, generously kitted out for guests to cook and settle in, while the farm shop stocks a wide range of organic delicacies selected from local producers, small breweries, cheesemakers, and coffee roasters. Rosso even offers its own house wine, made by an organic winery in Lake Constance.

The retreat is surrounded by a garden that grows wild in summer and provides many fruits and vegetables year-round, and there are chickens pecking away in the courtyard. Attentive to local resources, Rosso was renovated using only natural materials. "We are very conscious of every decision we make. Our energy comes from regenerative sources, our heating system works with wood, and we have installed solar panels on the roof," the owners say.

OPPOSITE   Looking toward a communal sun terrace at the rear of the house, with the retreat's fragrant herb garden in the foreground.

ABOVE The spacious kitchen/dining area in the apartment dubbed La Famiglia. All of the rooms are tall and bright with exposed wooden beams and lime plaster.

Every once in a while, the couple invites a chef over to cook dinner for guests and neighbors. In winter, they feast for long hours and in summer an outdoor pizza oven is heated up to enjoy lunch on the terrace. For Christian and Lisa, the sense of community prevails, opening a door to a richer life. "Rosso is just very personal: it's like a family house you can be part of for a while," Lisa adds.

ABOVE   The rooms at Rosso exude rustic charm, with chunky wooden country tables, earthenware pots, and meadowscape flower arrangements.

Domaine de la Trigalière

A Forward-Thinking Forest Estate

AMBILLOU
|
TOURAINE
|
FRANCE

Set within hundreds of hectares of preserved nature, forests, and ponds in the French province of Touraine, Domaine de la Trigalière is an impressive vacation destination centered around an 1830s chateau with 14 additional country homes and former farm buildings. Renovated over the decades by three generations of the Cheuvreux family, 16 accommodations offer self-catering facilities in both central and remote parts of the estate for short- and long-term country stays. Ranging in size and style—from a stylish barn to a timeless peasant's home or an elegant brick abode—they house from 2 to 18 people.

Around the gites, the property is rich with vegetable gardens, stables, an old gardener's house, and endless pathways heading into deep forests. Nature creates a wonderful playground in which guests can explore, forage, fish, walk, forest bathe, and wind down. "Inside the domaine, the idea is to get lost, explore, discover a tree, spot a wild animal: it's all about disconnecting from the urban life to reconnect to nature and childhood memories. I want to embrace those past souvenirs in a contemporary way," says Aleksandra Cheuvreux.

"It was quite a leap to open the family estate to the public, to share our passion, values, and vision," continues Aleksandra, who now runs Domaine de la Trigalière. It was her grandfather who purchased the property seven decades ago with the desire to bring man and nature together. Aleksandra's father Bruno subsequently took over. With the same desire to create a legacy, he set up an 8-hectare (20-acre) oak tree arboretum (one of Europe's largest), to protect different species for generations to come.

OPPOSITE   One of two houses that make up La Beausserie. Typical of an 18th-century French farmhouse, the cottage has a steep tiled roof and sloping walls.

TOURAINE
FRANCE

078

ABOVE   La Maison d'Annie, la Maison des Enfants, and la Dreuserie comprise a run of three beautifully renovated cottages with shuttered windows and cottage gardens.

ABOVE While the gîtes and suites at Domaine de la Trigalière are housed in very different buildings, the interiors are all simply kitted out with country-style furnishings and fabrics.

TOURAINE
FRANCE

080

ABOVE   At the heart of a stay here is the forest.
Diners are encouraged to dine al fresco and to master
the art of forest bathing.

With climate change, certain endemic oaks are struggling to adapt; by collecting species from the same latitude around the world, Bruno sought to build resilience through biodiversity—the antithesis of how forests have been exploited for decades.

"We don't consider ourselves as hoteliers: our journey is one of trial and error. Remaining true to ourselves and our family values is key. Our goal is to protect nature, offer visitors a quiet haven, and welcome tomorrow in a sustainable, innovative way," says Aleksandra. "My father recently built a photovoltaic farm on the property: it provides the domain with clean, local energy and helps further protect our forest, which has never been as healthy!" she concludes.

ABOVE   At Domaine de la Trigalière, life can be as simple as packing a basket with a picnic lunch and taking a boat out on one of the estate's ponds.

Grace & Savour, Hampton Manor

This Country Hotel Curates a Stay from the Ground Up

HAMPTON IN ARDEN | WARWICKSHIRE | UK

Grace & Savour is a five-room hotel complete with a soil-to-table restaurant. All of the rooms at the hotel, as well as the restaurant itself, open onto the Walled Garden from which many of the kitchen's raw ingredients are harvested. Owners James and Fjona Hill aim to both surprise and educate their guests with spectacular meals by chef David Taylor and day-time demonstrations devised and orchestrated by his Norwegian wife, Anette. The joint aim of the two couples is to demonstrate that good farming is the secret to real flavor.

This boutique hotel is a new venture at the larger Hampton Manor, a monumental residence built in 1855 for Prime Minister Sir Robert Peel. The historic house, along with 18 hectares (45 acres) of land, has been run by James's family for three generations. With its promise to deliver a truly immersive experience, Grace & Savour adds a new contemporary twist. "We want to celebrate this movement in growing and farming that is shifting away from the industrial model towards a more diverse, naturally resilient future," chef David explains. "The underlying belief is that what our farming communities are ultimately yielding is not only more nutrient-rich food but more flavorful."

While serving as part of the Michelin-starred Maaemo team in Oslo, chef David learned about the need to nurture strong relationships with producers and farmers. Back in the United Kingdom, he visited a number of farmers and fishermen to select those working sensitively in their environments, using a range of practices including rewilding, diversification, agroforestry, organic principles, and biodynamic farming.

OPPOSITE Hampton Manor is the epitome of the English country house, filled with neoclassical furniture in sumptuous textiles in rich colors—the height of good taste.

WARWICKSHIRE
UK

TOP   The taste of summer on a plate—one of chef David Taylor's outstanding creations with ingredients harvested from the garden.

BOTTOM   Dr. Sally Bell

With extensive glass doors, the restaurant opens onto the Walled Garden, which produces an acre of food using organic principles. The growing program is overseen by family member and lifestyle medicine specialist Dr. Sally Bell, who was also key in connecting the garden to the GRFFN Project (Growing Real Food for Nutrition), a UK-wide initiative that looks at how growing methods affect nutrient density. Adjacent to the Walled Garden is a bakery run by artisan baker Min Go, who also supplies bread to Grace & Savour. Having trained at Meyers Bageri in Copenhagen, she brings her expertise and passion for ancient and indigenous varieties of grain to the estate. Open to the local community, the coffee shop creates a natural bonding place for those passionate about good taste, great produce, creative talent, and local agriculture.

ABOVE A table at Grace & Savour, the estate's soil-to-table restaurant overlooking the Walled Garden where much of the fresh produce is grown.

WARWICKSHIRE
UK

086

ABOVE   Looking down on the impressive estate at Hampton Manor, nestled among the trees in the heart of the stunning Warwickshire countryside.

Hotel Crillon le Brave

A Historic Hamlet Reimagined as a Contemporary Lifestyle Hotel

VAUCLUSE
|
PROVENCE
|
FRANCE

Nestled in a listed secular village on top of a hill, Hotel Crillon le Brave has medieval flair: the decor within its 18 suites and 16 rooms hints at the timeless beauty of Provence with old stone walls, red-tiled floors, earthy materials, and essential crafts. The hotel's large terraces are home to a bar and seasonal restaurant inspired by the exceptional surroundings: vineyards, orchards, vegetable gardens, and fields of flowers.

Facing Mont Ventoux, the hotel comprises a dozen original houses that date back to the 16th and 17th centuries, all connected to one another via a labyrinth of cobblestone alleys, terraces, and stairs. The part of the village that the hotel occupies was known in Roman times as Crillonium, named for one of Henry IV's fiercest generals during the Wars of Religion that swept through France in the late 16th century. A slice of French history, the fortified hamlet was abandoned and fell into decline.

When British couple Peter Chittick and Carolyn Fairbairn acquired the site, its buildings were in ruins. Painstakingly, they brought them back to life. Today, herb gardens, towering cypress trees, roses, and climbing vines have turned the hotel terraces into a cascading garden. More recently, the Pariente family took over with the aim to protect and preserve the hotel, modernizing it only where needed. "We kept the old white stones to preserve the historical landmark and will go miles to pass this incredible heritage to future generations," explains Leslie Kouhana Pariente, who leads the family group. Together with interior architect Charles Zana, the Parientes transformed the interiors, introducing a minimal palette, ceramics, vintage

OPPOSITE   Hotel Crillon le Brave is like a village within a village. So successful is the renovation here that the hotel blends seamlessly with its surroundings.

PROVENCE
FRANCE

090

ABOVE   Bedrooms at the hotel are decorated in an understated style, with pretty textiles and colors that echo those found in the Provencal landscape.

HOTEL CRILLON LE BRAVE

furniture, and paintings to create sophisticated rural interiors inside the beautiful vaulted rooms.

Local traditions are revived through food, wine experiences, and cultural journeys in and around Provence. Visitors are invited to tour medieval villages, visit artist studios, and lavender fields in season. Inspired by the richness of the terroir of Provence, the hotel's chef Adrien Brunet selects products sourced from the best neighboring producers: for him, the essence of a recipe is not to transform the product, but to reveal its original taste. "Come with me," says Adrien, "I'll guide you through the neighboring hills, take you on a journey to meet wonderful producers and winemakers who have such a respect for the seasons and their terroir!"

ABOVE   Guests staying at the Crillon le Brave have a host of spa treatments available to them, as well as a heated outdoor swimming pool.

Mezi Plůtky

A Light-Filled Countryside Stay

ČELADNÁ
|
MORAVIA-SILESIA
|
CZECH REPUBLIC

Hidden in the middle of the Beskids, a high range in the Carpathian Mountains of the Czech Republic, lies Mezi Plůtky, a 200-year-old house surrounded by meadows and impressive trees. In recent years, the house has been fully renovated to create four en suite bedrooms and a large communal kitchen/living space in which guests can gather around the fire after a hard day's hiking.

Mezi plůtky can be translated from the Czech to mean "in between fences," a nod toward the many wooden fences farmers traditionally installed in the rural region. Having seen potential for a hospitality opportunity, local hotel and restaurant owner Daniela Hradilová set about giving the house a new lease on life. She repaired the original wooden roof, stabilized old structural beams, and brought much needed light into the building. One by one, she turned small windows into larger openings and added skylights to bring in direct sunlight from above. Daniela also converted a barn into a winter garden and a summer bedroom. The entire renovation process drew on the immediate environment—locally sourced stone and wooden elements reclaimed from abandoned cottages. Structures were repaired or replaced using traditional methods: "Working with this philosophy in mind was key for me: it helps deliver a better aesthetic while keeping costs low and caring for future generations," explains Daniela.

Inside the house, Daniela painted the wooden beams white and laid pale stone floors. She covered the walls in smooth gypsum plaster and installed a minimalist oak staircase that runs all the way to the attic. To complement the traditional craftsmanship, Daniela introduced elements of contemporary

OPPOSITE   Looking across the tranquil pond toward the beautifully renovated country house, with whitewashed walls and newly tiled roof.

MORAVIA-SILESIA
CZECH REPUBLIC

094

ABOVE The scale of this lofty bedroom is magnified by the use of white on the ceiling boards and beams. Minimal, small-scale furnishings emphasize the effect.

design to Mezi Plůtky's generous, open-plan suites. Scandinavian-style furnishings, free-standing bathtubs, and natural textiles set the tone in a low-key brown, gray, and white color palette. Bringing people together, the public area is an inviting space with a lofty living room and kitchen in which to enjoy sipping South Moravian wines or regionally brewed Czech beer while eating healthy nibbles prepared using locally farmed ingredients.

ABOVE Daniela's monochrome palette and minimalist furnishings bring a timelessness to the rooms of the house. Materials are natural and limited to wood, stone, plaster, and cane.

Ansitz Hohenegg

A Renovated Alpine Refuge in the Bavarian Alps

GRÜNENBACH
IM ALLGÄU
|
BAVARIA
|
GERMANY

Set in the Allgäu Alps, between Bregenz and Kempten, Ansitz Hohenegg is an original 1724 cottage that has been converted into four luxury apartments catering specifically to large groups and families. Standing in a clearing surrounded by spruce forests, the retreat is accessible through a small path up the Hohenegg hills and, in winter, when the landscape is covered in snow, it has the feel of a remote mountain refuge.

The cottage was restored and modernized by Anna-Dina and Sebastian Priller, who found a way to escape their own too-busy lives in Augsburg through this project. While preserving the building's traditional character, the couple has introduced contemporary architectural features to bring it up to date. Ranging from 60 to 290 square meters (645 to 3,120 square feet), each apartment is equipped with a fireplace, a well-appointed kitchen, and Alpine-inspired objects. Interior furnishings are in harmony with nature and focus on materials that age gracefully, such as leather, woolen textiles, wood, and stone. Wall-mounted antlers, checkered bed linen, and traditional corner benches contribute to the Alpine theme.

On a day-to-day basis, Anna-Dina and Sebastian collaborate with local chefs, craftsmen, and producers: meals can be ordered from local family-owned restaurants and beers are from the nearby Riegele brewery, founded in 1386. Overall, their ethos has been to think about future generations: "What can we do and build today that they will genuinely benefit from?" Anna-Dina and Sebastian explain. For guests, Ansitz Hohenegg offers the perfect hideaway in which to recharge the batteries. On the grounds a sauna

OPPOSITE Looking down on the retreat surrounded by spruce trees, it is easy to see the appeal for guests seeking a break totally immersed in nature.

BAVARIA
GERMANY

ABOVE   There is a sense of slowing down at Ansitz Hohenegg.
There are no distractions other than the sights and sounds
of nature: rustling trees, birdsong, and a distant waterfall.

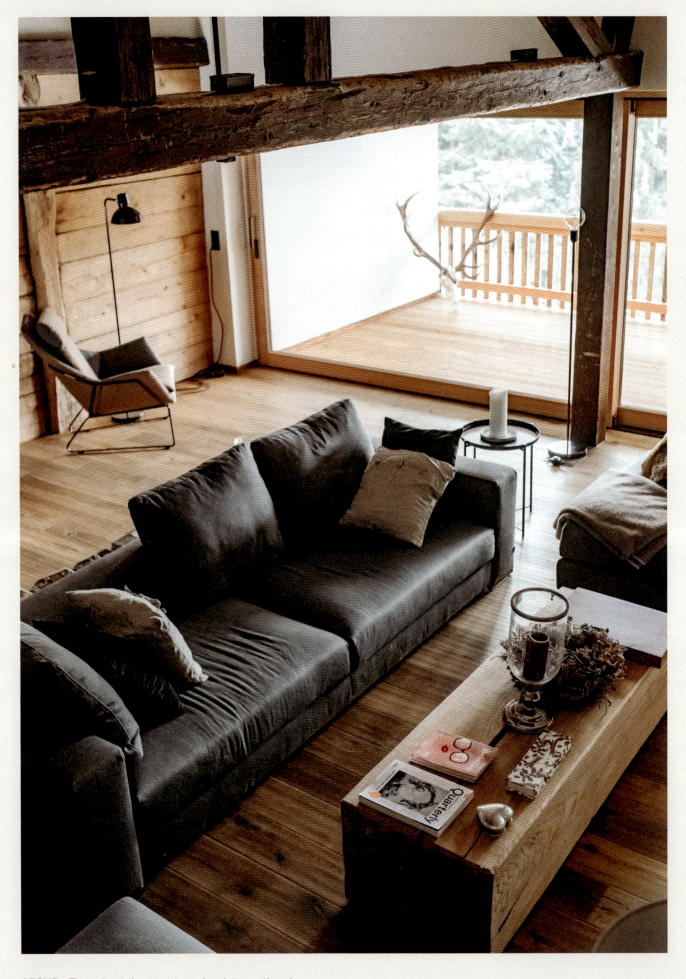

ABOVE   Throughout the retreat, modern interventions have been introduced carefully to preserve and enhance the character of the place. Furnishings are minimalist and natural.

built using local hand-planed spruce wood offers the ultimate relaxation and can be used either as a Finnish or organic steam sauna fragrant with soothing or invigorating local herbs. In the immediate surroundings, the forest offers a vast playground to be explored year-round by bike, on skis, or on foot. "Here, many guests feel they reconnect with their inner child: they find they want to play in the woods and enjoy days in slow motion. Some really wish they didn't have to head back to a busy urban life," adds Anna-Dina.

ABOVE   A judicious selection of furnishings and fittings combines with a warm color palette to create spaces that are cozy and restful.

Unpacking the Power of Local Communities

By supporting and celebrating all that is local, a new generation of hospitality venues is becoming integral to the cultural and economic fabric of remote and rural places.

There is a current trend for new hoteliers to choose remote and regional locations for their hotels, retreats, and guesthouses, where they focus specifically on the importance of the location and its community. The aim is to support and celebrate the culture of the community they have joined rather than simply to profit from it. These hoteliers seek active ways to contribute to the culture and economy of their new surroundings. They welcome members of the local community through workshops, events, and festivals. They provide employment opportunities, showcase local growers and makers, and encourage others to do the same. A handful of these new hoteliers go even further, working with community-run models that directly generate profit for the community.

In the remote village of Saint Nicolas de Véroce near Chamonix, France, winter nights are long, dark, and cold. But, at 3:00, light can be shining through the window of Hotel L'Armancette's bakery, where a team of three bakes bread for hotel guests and the local village. Renovated with care, this old Alpine chalet has brought more than a few luxury rooms to the traditional hamlet. The bakery, also part coffee shop, part tearoom, is where the villagers gather—from the elderly to children, ski instructors, local bus drivers, and hikers.

The owners of L'Armancette recently renovated another chalet to create Le Mont Joly, a bistro, bar, and lounge that serves local specialties and is bustling with locals year-round. Daily, a swarm of regional cheesemakers, winemakers, and producers deliver fresh produce to L'Armancette's restaurant; local teenagers apply for seasonal jobs; nearby farmstays renovate rooms to welcome guests attracted by the village's rejuvenation; skilled physiotherapists and yoga teachers in the valley find an additional income working shifts at the hotel. Playing an essential role in the village today, L'Armancette has created a virtuous ecosystem, essential to the area's cultural and economic viability.

Vital to supporting and celebrating regional traditions, conscious rural hotels also have the power to revive local communities in an economic sense, by providing direct and indirect job opportunities through their venture. When considered wisely, money spent by such venues serves as an investment in the community, from the local farmer whose produce ends up on the table at the hotel restaurant to the tradesmen whose expertise is relied upon for its construction.

"Hotels are like small cities; they need many talents to operate," explains Eric Dardé, of Le Moulin in France. "If run consciously, they have the power to change, impact and/or greatly benefit their immediate surroundings." Eric is the founder of the hotel group

ABOVE   Auberge de La Maison, a traditional chalet at the foot of Mont Blanc in Courmayeur, France, has been run by the same family for three generations.

Beaumier, which transforms old properties into hotels and retreats with flair and respect for local traditions. "It is our responsibility to protect local heritage for future generations," he continues. "We don't want to change the way an old village functions—on the contrary, we want to bring lost customs back. So many touristic regions have modernized too quickly, embraced quick wins, and turned their back to traditions. By doing so, many have lost their soul and identity."

Bringing together guests and villagers is key in creating the right dynamic. Generous and community-minded, a new generation of rural stays open their doors to locals: a new soft power emerges through such community engagement, and helps to revive such destinations. At The Glen Wilde in the Catskills, USA, 17 modernist bungalows dating from the 1940s, have been renovated to welcome a new generation of nature-loving guests. Linked to the neighboring town via a small trail through the woods, the lodge interacts as much as possible with local retailers, producers, and restaurateurs: they come to cater for guests, delivering meals or produce that can be barbecued. The relationship is mutually beneficial.

The power to change people's outlook on life is fundamental in the hospitality industry, and several hoteliers have found that it can be a real eye-opener to run artist residencies. "Art and artists have the capacity to instigate social change and offer new perspectives on contemporary issues," says Zita Cobb, founder of Fogo Island Inn, set on an island in remote Newfoundland. Running artist residencies since 2008, the Fogo Island Arts (FIA) organization supports research, production, and exchange for creatives in all fields from around the world. "Fogo Island itself represents society on a small scale: all the challenges of our digital world, our fraught relationships to the natural world, our integration within global economic, social, and political currents are present here in a condensed form," explains Zita. "What is also at play during each and every residency is the way culture is shared with local islanders: profound connections

ABOVE   Family time is paramount at Nimmo Bay, Canada. Here a family gets acquainted with the traditional Canadian board game crokinole.

are born with our close-knit community." Inside the lodge, the art gallery exhibits the works of residents: accessible to all, it welcomes villagers and guests alike.

Villa Lena in Tuscany, Italy, also runs a not-for-profit organization that invites artists in residence to collaborate with the local community. For example, New York street artist Chris "Daze" Ellis worked with schoolchildren in the nearby village of Palaia to create a mural. For the piece, entitled *Quest for Knowledge*, the pupils of the local school used spray paint to explore themes relating to nature and science. "The process nurtures both the artists and the local community," explains owner Lena Evstafieva, a former art-world professional and collector. "On the estate, the artist residency coexists with the Villa Lena hotel, restaurant, and agricultural domain. Resident artists become part of the community life, participating in the agricultural activities such as the grape harvest for wine, olive harvest for oil, and truffle hunting in fall. The exchange isn't only artistic, it's a two-way street: we learn from them and they learn from local makers and the natural surroundings," shares Lena.

Blurring the lines between guest house and artist residency, Casa Balandra in Majorca has six shared studio spaces, plus six guest rooms. "Our approach is community based: we encourage a group of creatives from different fields to exchange ideas and work," sister-owners Isabella and Claudia del Olmo explain. "The feeling of community that is created when working side by side, cooking, and eating together has the power to change individuals," they add.

Fostering change, a handful of hoteliers choose festivals to gather communities and share knowledge. Through its Light Series Events, Greek Dexamenes Seaside Hotel has featured light sculptures in its

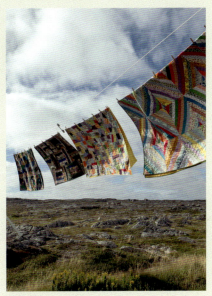

ABOVE   At Fogo Island Inn in Newfoundland, Canada, each bed is spread with a locally crafted quilt.

ABOVE   "The Story of Gardening," an educational exhibition at The Newt in Somerset, UK.

BELOW Fostering the artist community at Casa Balandra in Mallorca, Spain (top left) and Villa Lena in Tuscany, Italy (top right and bottom). Artists collaborate with each other and the community.

silo, held an architecture exhibition in collaboration with the Mies van der Rohe Foundation, and hosted a series of talks with architects called "Tank Readings" related to light, nature, and the Mediterranean landscape. It also organizes art and craft workshops that bring guests, friends, families, and the local community together. "Sharing and learning is key," says founder Nikos Karaflos, and creator of the cultural program. "For example, we organize a Mediterranean Garden workshop with a local naturalist, who has set up a seed bank of nongenetically modified local species. Such initiatives benefit all: it empowers the local community, brings knowledge forward, and acts for future generations," Nikos adds.

Beyond cultural programs, festivals, and artist residencies, a handful of conscious hospitality owners are bringing life back into remote areas. Their presence cements the local community, brings new opportunities, and creates jobs. Deep in the Carpathian Mountains of Romania, Șesuri is literally run by villagers. Since 2005, German owners Volker Bulitta and Lilli Steier have worked together with farmers and hospitality experts, carpenters, and builders to renovate a series of vernacular houses that now comprise a hotel. The collaboration is so fruitful that they have started a furniture business together with skilled craftspeople from the area, selling bespoke pieces across Europe. Empowering the local community and introducing a new stream of wealth, Șesuri is a great example of reciprocal hospitality. It thrives because of its relationship with the community: a win-win scenario.

TOP   After 30 years in the making, a rural vacation at Ebbio feels like visiting old friends.

BOTTOM   The Soares family of Malhadinha Nova has been contributing to the local community for 40 years.

Also exemplary is the business model of Fogo Island Inn. Set on a remote island off the edge of Newfoundland, the hotel is run by Shorefast, a Canadian charity founded in 2004 by eighth-generation Fogo Islanders: Zita, Alan, and Anthony Cobb. The aim of the foundation is to ensure a stable economic future for Fogo Island and other similar rural communities around the world. On an operational level, this means that there is no private benefit: all surplus income from the Fogo Island Inn is reinvested in the local community. Geared toward community development and cultural preservation, the inn's strict sourcing policies ensure that local suppliers are favored for food, amenities, and third-party services. Seafood and fish are harvested in the waters around Fogo Island, thus supporting local fishermen, while as a whole, 80 percent of ingredients used are fished, farmed, hunted, or harvested locally in Newfoundland. The inn's furniture was handcrafted and produced on Fogo Island, employing local artisans and makers and helping one of Canada's oldest communities become economically resilient.

In Greenland, the opening of Ilimanaq Lodge has embraced the village's social issues and stopped the community's slow decline. Extreme, the arctic destination had 80 inhabitants back in 2010, which fell to a little over 50 in a decade. Creating a lodge to first save and then sustain the local community was instigated by three parties: the Danish foundation Realdania By & Byg, the local Qaasuitsup Municipality, and conscious operator World of Greenland. Coming together with the aim to create jobs and embrace traditions, the proactive trio restored two 17th-century buildings erected by the first settlers; they improved the village's infrastructure; and they created fifteen modern, sustainable cabins for tourists. "Ilimanaq Lodge clearly saved the local community from depopulation," says Asger Køppen, World of Greenland's director. "Hopefully, this project can change the way we look at tourism development in the future."

THE POWER OF COMMUNITY

109

OPPOSITE   At L'Ovella Negra Mountain Lodge in Andorra, Prisca Llagostera urges her guests to master "the art of doing nothing."

ABOVE   At Dr. Kavvadia's Organic Farm in Corfu, Greece, age-old methods are used to harvest olives for producing oil.

Ebbio

Community Lies at the Heart of This Italian Agro Retreat

MONTERIGGIONI
(SIENA)
|
TUSCANY
|
ITALY

"My mother had this huge dream," says Sibilla de Vuono, "and along the way, her dream also became mine." Nestled in the heart of Tuscany, Ebbio is the story of a mother and a daughter, Frances Bevilacqua and Sibilla de Vuono, who turned the ruins of a 13th-century farmhouse into an organic and sustainable destination with ten bedrooms surrounded by 7 hectares (17 acres) of countryside.

"When my mother bought the place in 1989, she was fleeing Naples and urban life," explains Sibilla. "She wanted to live in harmony with nature, respect the seasons, and live sustainably—surrounded by people who felt the same." Sibilla remembers her mother being "different." Different she was, for she was a true visionary: she imagined Ebbio as a place to heal and gather, reconnect and disconnect. Over the years, Ebbio became a place of retreat, and more.

Following a career in fashion, Sibilla took over in 2016. At first, she feared she would miss the vibrancy of city life. The opposite happened. She accepted all the imperfections of a working farm and finally felt anchored. Nourished by a deeper connection to nature, she learned to let go. Sibilla reworked the 100-square-meter (1,076-square-foot) old stables as accommodations, using only organic materials and a natural color palette; she collected old furnishings and started placing family heirlooms in individual rooms. She even decided to serve meals on her own collection of Ginori plates: "You put your best things out to celebrate your guests. This is the Italian way of life!"

Thirty years in the making, Ebbio lives by the moto "ripe, fresh, in season, straight from the tree." If the retreat produces all the fruits and vegetables used

OPPOSITE Set within miles of unspoiled Tuscan countryside, this agro retreat offers a calm and tranquil space in which to experience traditional farming life.

ABOVE   There is an emphasis on being outside at Ebbio, whether working the land, taking part in a yoga class, or enjoying an al fresco meal.

in the kitchen, foraging brings additional surprises, such as porcini mushrooms, chanterelles, asparagus, or stinging nettles in season. Recipes are creative and traditions honored; from cooking workshops to food preservation, nothing goes to waste. Whether it is health, architecture, food, vegetable gardens, or simply nature, Ebbio brings everything full cycle, uplifting soul and spirit in the making.

With returning visitors who have since become house friends, life at Ebbio feels more like visiting an extended family than staying in a hotel. "Here, there is no branding, sometimes we give more than we earn, but we wouldn't do it any other way," says Sibilla.

ABOVE Served according to the maxim that "food is medicine," all meals at Ebbio are organic, vegetarian, and made with homegrown and locally sourced foods.

TUSCANY
ITALY

ABOVE AND PREVIOUS PAGE Inside the villa are 10 simply furnished bedrooms. Communal spaces include a sitting room with a traditional fireplace and a yoga hall.

ABOVE Rooms have a rustic vibe, with exposed beams, worn tiled floors, woven textiles, and windows that look out across the rolling Tuscan hills.

L'Armancette

A Luxury Hotel Reinvigorates an Alpine Village

SAINT-NICOLAS
DE VÉROCE
|
AUVERGNE-
RHÔNE-ALPES
|
FRANCE

Facing Mont Blanc, in the small Alpine village of Saint-Nicolas de Véroce, L'Armancette is not your typical 17-room luxury hotel and spa. The traditional wood and stone chalet sits in the middle of the village, in close proximity to a listed baroque church and old farm buildings. The main entrance welcomes guests, while an adjacent door sets the tone: a ski instructor comes to buy a baguette, two kids leave with *pains au chocolat*, and an old couple walks in slowly to sit down for tea. Before L'Armancette opened just a few seasons ago, there was very little happening in Saint-Nicolas de Véroce, but establishing this bakery at the center of the village changed the dynamic. Each morning at 3:00, three bakers get to work for the hotel and locals alike, preparing bread, pastries, tarts, and granola under the supervision of the hotel's pastry chef Florian Langellier and bread maker Pierre Souillé.

In June 2021, L'Armancette turned a former hotel into Le Mont Joly, a local bistro and bar, complete with a pool table, a lounge area with an open fireplace, and an upstairs terrace. Changing daily, a menu created by 25-year-old chef Thomas Giraudet offers homemade dishes and Alpine specialties prepared using local produce, such as Reblochon cheese, home-baked bread, trout fillets from Savoie, and local Chartreuse liqueur to replace rum in the traditional *baba au rhum*. Employing young local staff, working with producers in the area, and offering a place to celebrate, or simply share a drink in the evening, the hotel's presence has brought clear changes to this quiet little village.

Attracting connoisseurs, the hotel's gastronomic restaurant La Table d'Armante reaches sustainable

OPPOSITE   Rising from the rugged Alpine landscape, Le Mont Joly bistro has become a central hub for guests and locals alike.

AUVERGNE-RHÔNE-ALPES — FRANCE

ABOVE The hotel at the heart of L'Armancette's enterprise. Besides Le Mont Joly bistro, the enterprise includes an additional three chalets in the village.

summits. Led by chef Julien Darcy, guests are seated around custom-made solid wood tables designed by master craftsman Christophe Delcourt. Terroir rules as the chef works with all the best surrounding farms: cheese and milk products come from la Ferme des Roches Fleuries in the village; cold cuts and meats are bought in from Maison Baud in Villaz and in Megève; saffron is cultivated by Maryline Dupraz and Eric Schoder in Thonon-les-Bains, and fresh herbs are handpicked by the chefs during Alpine walks. All dishes are matched with local wines from Savoie, which add a local vibrancy to the cuisine. Respectfully anchored to the traditional village, luxury hotel L'Armancette has completely revitalized the locale via bread, pastries, local farmers, and pure Alpine spirit.

TOP   The wood-paneled pool room at Le Mont Joly.

BOTTOM   An exquisite raspberry tart on the dessert menu at the bistro, decorated with delicate violas.

Bovina Farm & Fermentory

A Homestead That Revisits Rural Traditions

BOVINA
|
NEW YORK
|
USA

Set in the Catskill Mountains, upstate New York, Bovina Farm & Fermentory is a rural homestead built like a house in the woods by Elizabeth Starks and Jacob Sackett. Designed as a place to gather, stay, eat, and drink, it houses a space for visitors to dine downstairs and stay in the inn upstairs.

For Elizabeth and Jacob, the homestead represents a return to their roots as barefooted kids, who grew up close to the land. For Jacob, the connection was deeper still: this rural project was a way to reconnect with a long family lineage of seven generations of Catskills farmers. "We decided that we would build a house in the woods and invite all of you in. We hope you'll take off your coat, join us around the table, and stay awhile," say Jacob and Elizabeth, generously.

Every day, the pair of them are busy imagining the ideal farmstay, but also tending to vegetable gardens, orchards, and free-ranging animals. Celebrating all things local, Jacob and Elizabeth oversee all food and drinks served: meals are homemade using ingredients that are attentively sowed, raised, and harvested by the couple or local farmers, and beers are brewed in a traditional fashion using grains grown in local fields and malted in a barn in a neighboring town. In addition, a small flock of sheep raised on the farm brings fresh sheep's cheese and yogurt to the table. Working with the bounty the surrounding wilderness offers, Jacob and Elizabeth handpick every ingredient, and curate every object: "Our homestead is run only by the two of us. It creates an intimacy that can only be achieved when so few hands are at play; every detail of the craft we know so well, be it planting, harvesting, cooking, brewing, or building," the couple explains.

OPPOSITE   Life at Bovina Farm & Fermentory revolves around a traditional Catskills timber-clad farmhouse, complete with a substantial porch.

ABOVE   Elizabeth sets the table for lunch. There is a great emphasis here on slow living and sharing experiences with others out of doors.

NEW YORK
USA

124

ABOVE AND OPPOSITE   Inside the farmhouse, a generous
dining room has the vibe of a Shaker-style refectory.
Simple, seasonal home-cooked meals are the usual fare.

"Being so rural pushed us to create a space that offers everything guests need right here focusing on genuine, raw experiences with slow living in mind," they add. Slow living, for example, entails not offering food to go because the couple believes meals are a ritual to be shared and enjoyed slowly and in the company of others or in nature. The pair also encourage guests to shut down phones and computers, allowing them to better enjoy the present moment. At Bovina Farm & Fermentory, no stay is complete without a joyful dinner table: in the heart of the Catskills, the experience feels like a reunion with kindred spirits at a friend's place.

ABOVE AND OPPOSITE   Catering for small groups of people allows owners Elizabeth Starks and Jacob Sackett to run the retreat on their own, sharing their dream with guests.

L'Ovella Negra Mountain Lodge

An Alpine Lodge Turns Everyday Life into a Celebration

INCLÈS VALLEY | ANDORRA

Tucked at the end of Andorra's Inclès Valley at an altitude of 1,700 meters (5,580 feet), L'Ovella Negra is, as its name suggests, a perfect black sheep. The former tractor-shed-turned-modern-mountain-lodge resembles an Alpine refuge with a Scandinavian edge and wabi-sabi interior. Think: concrete walls, woolen blankets, wooden communal tables, old plank floors and chairs, brass candlesticks, and soft light, all set around a central fireplace in a room furnished with vintage leather armchairs and velvet sofas. Guests access the six rooms on the second floor via a sleek open staircase. Minimal and essential, each room celebrates natural materials and has views across the valley to the mountains.

L'Ovella Negra is an Alpine playground where family members and friends get together for a meal or a concert. "I wanted to bring back a sense of community," says founder and manager, Prisca Llagostera. On a day-to-day basis, she promotes her own version of *dolce far niente*, the art of doing nothing, to all visitors as a way to embrace the moment, share it around hearty local food, and enjoy the surrounding nature.

In winter, when the valley is blanketed in snow, L'Ovella Negra gets cozy inside and the Lodge Canteen takes center stage. Local chef Sergi Simó, previously at Nerua Guggenheim Bilbao, and Martin Urrutia, formerly of Compartir Restaurant in Cadaqués, imagine unique fireside meals based on local ingredients and Catalan traditions. Dishes include the Catalan *trinxat*, a combination of cabbage, black pudding, and potatoes (only in winter), mountain deer carpaccio, or sautéed artichokes with ham and quail eggs.

OPPOSITE The rustic lodge nestles at the end of a valley at the foot of the mountains—the perfect spot for venturing out on a trek in the rugged landscape.

INCLÈS VALLEY
ANDORRA

ABOVE   There is an emphasis on shared experiences at L'Ovella Negra, and guests come together at mealtimes to dine around a communal table.

L'OVELLA NEGRA MOUNTAIN LODGE

ABOVE   Winters in the Inclès Valley can be harsh—inside the lodge, guests find no end of cozy nooks in which to snuggle up under a blanket or around a fireplace.

INCLÈS VALLEY
ANDORRA

ABOVE   In the communal living room, leather sofas and lounge chairs are arranged around a wood-burning stove, all in rich, neutral tones.

L'OVELLA NEGRA MOUNTAIN LODGE

On winter weekends, the inviting wooden shack, with a fireplace and two communal tables, houses pop-ups—the perfect halt after your snowshoe hike or ski-mountaineering session. When the sun is back, the same space overflows with joyful people and energy throughout July and August when live music nights are organized. Many have simply learned to bring a blanket and find a spot in the field. Open air means the world to Prisca, who chose this secluded location for people to reconnect: "I think I see magic where nobody else does," she explains—which is true, as L'Ovella Negra is a most magical place.

TOP   Wrapped in dark timber, the bedrooms have a rustic appeal. Comfort is key here: soft, natural textiles and dim lighting set the tone.

Auberge de La Maison

In Courmayeur, the Past Is Alive and Well

COURMAYEUR
|
AOSTA
VALLEY
|
ITALY

At the foot of Mont Blanc in Courmayeur stands a local institution: run by the Garin family for three generations, this traditional chalet has stood the test of time, home to countless mountain stories and family souvenirs. Founded in 1996 by Leo and Patrizia Garin, Auberge de La Maison is a hotel, a wellness center, and a restaurant.

Known across the valley as a wonder-hospitality man, Leo began his career working in restaurants run by his parents, before opening one of his own in the 1960s. His restaurant, the famed Maison Filippo, served local recipes in a simple Alpine house—actually his father's home. Today, an elderly Leo recalls the high-end clientele of the restaurant: "The king of Spain, the queen of Denmark, the French president, Alpinists such as Maurice Herzog, jazzman Stan Getz, and actress Gina Lollobrigida all came to eat antipasti, pasta dishes, and flambé desserts."

Upon entering Auberge de La Maison, one is struck by the presence of each and every object. An old Alpine boot, rusted crampons, oil paintings of the summits surrounding the hotel, intricately embroidered tablecloths, old milking pots—Auberge de La Maison is a destination with a soul, a chalet that breathes all the charm and tradition of Alpine hospitality.

The house is a refuge in winter, offering protection from the harsh weather; in summer, when the surrounding fields are green and tables are spread outside, it becomes a grand house. Today, Auberge de La Maison is run by Alessandra Garin, an elegant *maîtresse de maison* and a mountain girl at heart: "Living well means discovering, enriching oneself, and sharing with beauty and kindness in mind,"

OPPOSITE Crafted from stone and wood in traditional chalet style, La Maison enjoys an archetypal valley position surround by verdant Alpine meadows.

AOSTA VALLEY
ITALY

134

ABOVE   After a day's skiing in winter, or exploring the local village of Courmayeur, nothing beats the warmth of an open fire in rooms furnished with comfortable sofas and vintage prints.

ABOVE   La Maison's bedrooms cater to all tastes. Some conjure the atmosphere of a mountain hut, with timber-lined walls and sheepskins. Others are more genteel, with floral linens.

AOSTA VALLEY
ITALY

136

ABOVE   The meadows surrounding the hotel provide tranquil spaces where guests can enjoy the pure mountain air and immerse themselves fully in the stunning Alpine landscape.

she explains. With beautifully slanted roofs, old paintings, fresh linen, and incredible views over the Aosta Valley or Mont Blanc's stark peaks and glaciers, each room is the epitome of an Alpine retreat.

Down at the restaurant, where some of Leo's infamous dishes remain on the menu, Auberge de La Maison has the taste and flavors of the Aosta Valley. "Our terroir is authentic and sincere: products are grown in our garden or chosen from dedicated local producers because we know and appreciate the value of simplicity and the taste of tradition," explains Alessandra. In winter, the unusual Valpellinentze soup with Mantuan pumpkin fondue can be found nowhere other than in the restaurant—the blessing of staying in the Garins' home.

ABOVE   Much of life at La Maison revolves around traditions. Guests can explore the history of the place and imagine its past through the owners' possessions and heirlooms.

Unearthing the Potential of the Land

Living in direct contact with their terroir, rural hoteliers embrace nature and revel in its seasonal flavors.

As lovers of food and nature, the new guard of hoteliers in rural areas expend a great amount of time and effort growing and sourcing high-quality produce. Choosing to live with the land rather than simply on it, they grow their own vegetables, fruits, and herbs, look after animals, learn about the local terroir, and collaborate with local farmers. These hospitality initiatives are working to reinvigorate not just the communities that they are a part of, but the very land they occupy through agritourism and farm-to-table concepts for their hotel restaurants. Together with farmers, gardeners, and some Michelin-starred chefs, these hotels are establishing a new type of agriculture that is feeding into an exciting rural cuisine.

Picture the perfect vegetable garden: alleys of green sprouting vegetables, beds of fresh herbs, flowers in bloom, and bees pollinating under the shade of an old tree. Cycling through stages across the seasons, the garden is never the same and never quite predictable. Here, manure replaces chemicals and biodiversity thrives, supported by surrounding orchards, olive trees, and vineyards. In a nutshell, a complete ecosystem is at play. This garden is what many chefs, producers, naturalists, and self-taught hoteliers have moved out of cities to create. At the helm of this new agricultural and food movement are hospitality venues: farmstays, guesthouses, and hotels.

Leading the charge are chefs working in areas where the land has been degraded by farming over time. Sharing their experience around the table and in the fields, they naturally add a few rooms for guests to stay longer and connect deeply with the land. This is the case of Grace & Savour at Hampton Manor near Coventry in England, which has combined a five-suite retreat with a walled garden and a farm-to-table restaurant led by chef David Taylor.

On a day-to-day basis, David collaborates with Dr. Sally Bell who oversees the estate's growing program. The 18-hectare (45-acre) estate is a part of the GRFFN Project (Growing Real Food for Nutrition), a UK-wide initiative that looks at how growing methods affect nutrient density. For Bell, agriculture is about understanding the complexities of produce, taking into account broken food chains and the alarming scarcity of nutrient-rich soil. "Watching the manor garden come to life, I realized I had never looked far enough upstream to ask where our food comes from," says Sally. "I had no idea how broken the food system was. This led me to all these questions: is there a different way of producing food

ABOVE Heckfield Place, where fresh, seasonal food for the restaurants is grown on the estate's home farm.

ABOVE At Daylesford Longhouse in Victoria, Australia, a boutique farm, garden kitchen, cooking school, reception venue, and home all occupy a single 110-meter-long (360-foot-long) shed.

that is phenomenally nutritious and does nature good?"

This change of mindset and desire to better protect the land can be seen in rural hospitality venues in the United Kingdom and across the world where the land has been extensively farmed. At Heckfield Place in Hampshire, Culinary Director Skye Gyngell wants to connect the outside and the inside worlds through seasonal recipes that reflect the moment we are in. Like a winemaker, she works to express the qualities of the soil—for each landscape is unique. "Heckfield is really about showcasing nature's miracles and us reflecting that," she says.

Yet, for all of the shoots, flowers, and heirloom varieties to come to life, rich with flavors and nutrients, the Heckfield's agriculture had to be completely rethought. Previously farmed using pesticides and fertilizers, it took almost a decade to replenish the soil and return the land to a place where biodynamic farming principles reign. In 2020, Heckfield Place became certified organic, and in 2021 it achieved biodynamic status. "We experimented constantly to learn about the local terroir," Skye explains. "Now, looking back, we've seen incredible improvement in soil health and growth."

In other remote corners of the world, rural hotels are tackling the sheer difficulty of growing food. Following a stellar international career, Norwegian chef Halvar Ellingsen decided to establish Kvitnes farm, a 15-room farm hotel and restaurant, situated in Norway's arctic north. Working only with what the garden and nature have to offer, the menu at Kvitnes is entirely dependent on the land's resilience, growing cycles, and changing weather patterns. "Unlike many restaurants, we depend on a natural life cycle," explains Halvar. "We don't force anything onto the land, and we certainly don't set the guidelines: nature does. Everything is different here. The land doesn't provide us with the same ingredients. Here vegetables in late spring and summer have up to 24 hours of daylight; their taste is all the more intense and sweeter. Nothing compares to them."

Across the world, people are working to increase regional biodiversity. In the hospitality industry, many look to Michelin-starred chef Alain Passard, who took the culinary world by surprise in 2001 when he decided to feature only vegetables on the menu. Today, Passard cultivates more than 500 varieties of vegetables across his three farms in France, each bringing a particular richness to his menus.

Following the same approach, and with low-impact farming techniques, chefs like Cybèle Idelot of Domaine les Bruyères and Bertrand Grébaud of D'un Ile, have returned to the French countryside to establish restaurants and small guesthouses inspired by the landscape. On Inis Meáin in a guesthouse and restaurant that share the island's name, Michelin-starred chef Ruairí de Blacam strives to source everything from the sea and grounds, revealing the richness of this remote ecosystem. In the richly storied North Adams, Massachusetts, celebrated chef Cortney Burns embraced locality to revive forgotten recipes at The Airport Rooms—the restaurant of TOURISTS.

Beginning a new era, such restaurants and hotels are promoting a new kind of lifestyle and a new kind of cuisine. "Sometimes naked and raw is the best expression of a produce," says La Donaira's chef Fredrik Andersson who runs the kitchen at the remote Andalusian rural retreat. Honest, unpretentious, yet delectable, this new rural cuisine is seasonal, hyperlocal,

ABOVE   For the new rurals at Inis Meáin (top) and Grace & Savour (bottom), providing the freshest local food, exquisitely cooked, is crucial to the experience of a visit to their retreats.

TOP   Rich pickings at Heckfield Place. One of two restaurants on the estate, Marle focuses on dishes served straight from the earth.

TOP RIGHT   Grace & Savour at Hampton Manor in Warwickshire, UK, promises guests an immersive dining experience with a 15-course menu.

RIGHT   For many, nothing beats the new rural experience of eating al fresco, overlooking the terroir from which the meal has been sourced, as here at Masseria Calderisi.

homegrown, and foraged. Moreover, it brings heirloom varieties and biodiversity forward.

Bringing the honesty of this new way of cooking into light, *Le Fooding*—an influential French guide to restaurants, chefs, and hotels—highlights talents that promote local and seasonal produce. As Editor-in-Chief Elisabeth Debourse explains, "Chefs who embrace a soil-to-table approach are not shy to use the same seasonal ingredient, the same timeless recipe, the same cooking technique. Even if the approach and philosophy are similar, every meal is fundamentally different: each dish and produce has the taste of the terroir, the rain, the wind, the exposure to the sun. It is like a wild bouquet of flowers: always wild, it's never twice the same."

Millenary Mediterranean recipes could be considered the same way. Homegrown tomatoes, olives, freshly baked bread, capers, olive oil, wild herbs, and fresh goat's cheese have been a staple of Mediterranean cuisine for centuries, from Turkey and Greece to Portugal and across North Africa. When served at The Rooster's farm-to-table restaurant in Antiparos, this meal tastes of Greece. At Parco dei Sesi on the Sicilian island of Pantelleria, it has the minerality of the volcanic soil, while at Malhadinha Nova, Portugal, it speaks about the aridity of the soil. Even in Ebbio, Tuscany, or Masseria Calderisi, Puglia, both in Italy, the altitude and proximity to the sea create contrasting flavors. Just as a natural wine lover knows that each bottle, although made from the same grape variety, encapsulates a terroir and its yearly weather patterns, the new rural foodies focus on variations in taste and flavor: they're after a unique experience, that of produce grown in a specific location.

Reconnecting with the roots of agriculture and taste is precisely what agritourism is about: it brings produce and guests together under one roof, providing the possibility to learn how to grow, harvest, and cook. Located in a small town in Tasmania's beautiful Derwent Valley, The Agrarian Kitchen

ABOVE   At The Agrarian Kitchen in New Norfolk, Australia, Rodney Dunn and his wife Séverine Demanet want diners to experience a true sense of place through the food they eat.

ABOVE AND OPPOSITE   A pasta masterclass run by the cooking school at Daylesford Longhouse. The venue regularly invites chefs, artisans, and bakers to lead classes.

does just that, starting with the word agrarian, which means that "relating to fields or lands." Here, *Gourmet Traveller*'s former food editor Rodney Dunn and his wife Séverine Demanet reconnect the kitchen with the land through their farm-based cooking school. "We wanted to recreate the agrarian system that predated the Industrial Revolution," they explain. "It was a subsistence farming system where farmers grew a range of food crops and animals that complemented each other. The gardens were looked after using organic principles (no chemicals or artificial fertilizers) and, back in the day, they grew so many heirloom varieties that vegetable gardens were a paradise for diversity." Today, the kitchen aims to replicate this model, with cooking classes geared toward raising awareness of sustainable living.

On the mainland of Australia, a similar venture that combines agriculture, cooking, education, and accommodations has been established in rural Victoria—the Daylesford Longhouse. Owners Trace Streeter and Ronnen Goren have created a space that celebrates food and cooking, animal husbandry, gardening, and self-sufficiency. At the cooking school, they regularly invite and partner with passionate food artisans, fermenters, chefs, cheesemakers, and bakers to learn, share, taste, and then repeat. Wisely, places like The Agrarian Kitchen or Daylesford Longhouse are training a generation of conscious consumers and travelers alike.

For all those playing a role in the new rural movement, coming back to the land is the only sustainable way forward. Caring for the terroir is part of their ethos: they share it with guests through wonderful meals and shared experiences around their farms and gardens. Moreover, they hope to rally many to their vision, to heal the land to a larger extent. "We've lost touch with the earth that supports and sustains us," says Skye Gyngell of Heckfield Place. "We need to come back to a stewardship of the land."

FOOD AND AGRITOURISM

145

TOP (RIGHT) AND ABOVE   At Daylesford Longhouse, there is an emphasis on helping people to rediscover the simple joys of cooking with fresh produce.

ABOVE   A waterfront table set for two at Nimmo Bay, Canada, complete with Persian rug and blankets for a unique outdoor dining experience.

Heckfield Place

A Historical Mansion Embraces a Biodynamic Farm

HECKFIELD | HAMPSHIRE | UK

An 18th-century Georgian family home restored to its historic origins, Heckfield Place sits at the heart of a bountiful, botanical 177-hectare (438-acre) estate in Hampshire, England, just an hour's drive from London. Inside the house and additional buildings in the grounds, this luxury interpretation of the country house hotel has 45 beautifully furnished rooms catering to a discerning clientele.

"We like to think of ourselves as a meeting point: a place for new ideas, new connections, and the passing seasons," says Skye Gyngell, an acclaimed Australian-born British chef who acts as the estate's culinary director. Resolutely natural, Heckfield Place has sustainability at its heart and a forward-thinking view of its relationship with the land. Walled gardens, a glass house, and a home farm provide fruit, vegetables, honey, and flowers for the rooms and restaurants. "Everything at Heckfield Place relates to nature—from the house itself, which is positioned to align with the movement of the sun, to the biodynamic farm and farm-to-fork restaurants, which constantly adapt to the weather and seasons," adds Skye, who oversees the menus of the two on-site restaurants Marle and Hearth. If Marle focuses on the excitement and immediacy of food served straight from the earth, Hearth is centered around an open fire, using classic cooking methods to celebrate the land. In the Moon Bar, cocktails use the freshest ingredients to breathe new life into old recipes.

Designed using natural materials and craftsmanship, the rooms at the hotel reflect the estate's countryside abundance, supplied as they are with flowers, fresh-picked fruits or dried nuts, homemade lemonade, and herbal teas. Over the last decade, Heckfield Place has

OPPOSITE Looking toward the majestic, lovingly restored Georgian mansion, across the immaculately kept grounds of this Hampshire estate.

ABOVE Though contemporary in style, the rooms and spaces at Heckfield Place feature furnishings that harmonize with the architectural style of the house.

ABOVE The interior of the mansion has been restored elegantly, with an emphasis on maintaining the building's innate character.

HAMPSHIRE
UK

ABOVE AND OPPOSITE (TOP)   Set within the upper walled garden, the glass house is the perfect place to enjoy a traditional English afternoon tea.

had clear ambitions: to reconnect a grand English house, its home farm, and the local community, to craft a place that stands out of time, seeks to impart wisdom, and inspire change. "Connected to the land and the soil, we act as modern-day custodians of this remarkable estate; here, we are rooted in the rhythms of slow time—we live at nature's speed," sums up Skye.

ABOVE   The walled garden. There is a great emphasis on being bound to the natural rhythms of nature and on building a self-sustaining relationship between the house and the land.

Domaine les Bruyères

A Garden Escape Led by a Chef-Turned-Hotelier

GAMBAIS
|
ÎLE-DE-FRANCE
|
FRANCE

Set on a vast estate in the Haute Vallée de Chevreuse, Domaine les Bruyères is a former 19th-century coaching inn brought back to life by chef Cybèle Idelot and her husband Frank Idelot, an entrepreneur. Surrounded by 1.4 hectares (3.5 acres) of land and vegetable gardens, the historical house has five rooms designed for foodies who want to discover the chef's talent and dine in her soil-to-table restaurant.

A San Francisco native, chef Cybèle fell in love with France at a young age and opened her first restaurant, La Table de Cybèle, near Paris in 2013. Committed to zero-waste, plant-based, conscious cuisine, she always wanted to cultivate her own fruit and vegetables. When looking for the ideal vegetable garden, she and Frank found Domaine les Bruyères and decided to convert it into a countryside inn. "From the beginning, we wanted to keep it intimate and traditional, influenced by the seasons, local produce, and craft," the pair explains. Today, they run the garden at Domaine les Bruyères according to the principles of permaculture; attentive to sun exposure, winds, and all that a "living soil" requires.

Cybèle embraces regenerative principles and bakes her own bread. She also tends to extensive orchards—cherries, pears, apples, prunes, pawpaw, figs, pomegranates, and kiwis are all grown on site—alongside Sichuan pepper, elderflower, bushes of red and black currant, and other fruits. As for vegetables, the list is equally impressive.

To compose her daily menu, Cybèle teams up with local farms and responsible producers: seasonal heirloom tomatoes with smoked aubergine, homegrown shiso leaves, tamarind, and buckwheat is just one of her

OPPOSITE   The coaching inn at the heart of the Domaine les Bruyères, its yellow stone walls and shuttered windows typical of 19th-century vernacular architecture.

ÎLE-DE-FRANCE
FRANCE

ABOVE The hotel restaurant, Ruche, is a destination eatery for foodies who come from far and wide to sample Cybèle Idelot's food.

DOMAINE LES BRUYÈRES

heavenly creations. Come dessert, a regional prune is sweetened with sorrel sorbet, meringue, and geranium mousse—All in season! The decoration of the five rooms upstairs is also seasonal, with hand-picked colors from a predominantly green palette. "I want guests to feel at home, as if in a friend's house, to breathe in, stroll through the garden, look at the bouquets we place here and there," Cybèle explains. Each room feels like a countryside retreat, and as guests relax upstairs, an amazing dish is always being prepared downstairs, while outside the gardens are blooming.

BOTTOM   An open fire sets a welcoming tone in the hotel lounge.

TOP   Just one of the exquisite dishes prepared by Cybèle using ingredients she has grown herself.

ÎLE-DE-FRANCE
FRANCE

ABOVE   At the heart of the *domaine* are the gardens. Designed to increase the area's biodiversity, they include a pond, a greenhouse, Cybèle's vegetable garden, and a beehive.

157

DOMAINE LES BRUYÈRES

ABOVE   Guests staying at the house are encouraged to slow down and relax among the daisies in the garden, fully immersed in the nature that surrounds them.

Dr. Kavvadia's Organic Farm

Timeless Traditions Continue in an 18th-Century Olive Oil Farm

TZAVROS | CORFU | GREECE

A 15-minute drive from Corfu town, Dr. Kavvadia's organic farm is a natural and sustainable island haven. Praised for its award-winning olive oil and organic farm products, the sustainable farm has embraced the spirit of slow living in recent years, converting farm buildings to provide accommodations with five bedrooms so that guests can stay within its stunning rural surroundings.

The farm's origins date back to the 18th century and the installation of a small olive press; growing on the land are centenarian olive trees, some dating back as far as 400 years to Venetian times. The estate became the home of Dr. Kavvadia in the mid-20th century, and it was with his vision that farm operations came to blend practices of permaculture and sustainable farming. Originally an orthopedic surgeon, Dr. Kavvadia started experimenting with farming techniques to improve the quality of the estate's olive oil. He believed that by using only natural ways of farming, the grove would produce superior olive oil with increased healing properties. Furthermore, seeking to preserve rare and local species, he reintroduced two lesser-known olive varieties, the Lianelia and Thiako, making them accessible worldwide in the process. Today, Dr. Kavvadia's organic farm is run by his grandson, Apostolos, who perpetuates the doctor's philosophy, albeit along modern lines. Dr. Kavvadia's olive trees, now organically certified, are still cultivated in the most natural ways in order to preserve the grove's ancient, natural ecosystem. From the picking to the bottling, all processes of making the olive oil are carried out by hand and the oil remains unparalleled in quality.

OPPOSITE Totally at home in its surroundings, the Olive Storage House is the oldest building on the farm. Today it serves as a two-bedroom farmstay with a private garden.

ABOVE Walking through the olive grove, through trees that have been growing here for more than 100 years, it is easy to get a sense of the estate's rich rural history.

BOTTOM Rooms inside the farmhouse combine rustic charm with state-of-the-art appliances.

TOP Outside, the farm's gardens are lush and immaculately kept.

CORFU
GREECE

ABOVE Guests visiting the old olive press learn how olive oil is made and can enjoy a tasting session with fresh vegetables grown on the farm.

Elsewhere on the estate, an early-19th-century olive storage house and the former stables have both been converted and modernized to provide accommodations for paying guests. Each property is self-catering and has its own private garden. Living the perfect farm life, guests can expect daily deliveries of fresh produce such as eggs, organic vegetables, and, of course, olive oil. They are welcome to visit the old press and discover how the oil is made. And no stay is complete without a tasting session or a cooking class in which guests become immersed in the timelessness of Greek traditions.

TOP   A jolly outdoor kitchen area with a pizza oven and grill is well-equipped for al fresco dining and is available for hire.

Castello di Vicarello

Old Stones Turned into a Luxury Farm Retreat

CINIGIANO
|
TUSCANY
|
ITALY

Set between Rome and Florence where Tuscany's rolling hills are largely untouched, the 12th-century Castello di Vicarello was first erected by the Republic of Siena some 900 years ago. Today, with nine individually designed suites, the castle stands at the heart of a 40-hectare (100-acre) estate surrounded by organic vineyards, olive groves, and farmland, and serves as a luxury farm-to-table retreat.

The property was first discovered by Carlo and Aurora Baccheschi-Berti in the early 1980s. At the time, the couple was living between Bali and Milan, both of them working in fashion textiles and antique furniture. On seeing the ruins of Castello di Vicarello in their dilapidated state, the pair became smitten with the place—so much so that they bought it and relocated their family to this largely unknown region of Maremma. The initial restoration of the castle took 12 years of hard work, with the stylish couple going to great lengths to bring the property back to its former glory, while protecting both its history and its surroundings. After 25 years and substantial investment, the castle is now fully restored and maintains a sustainable approach to living.

The running of the castle and its surrounding land is now the responsibility of the couple's three sons, Neri, Brando, and Corso. Keen to safeguard Tuscan flavors, the estate is rich with homegrown products. A dedicated team of gardeners grows more than 50 varieties of vegetables and 30 aromatic herbs, and looks after olive groves and an award-winning vineyard. In the restaurant kitchen, Chef Kevin Luigi Fornoni follows a farm-to-table approach, using

OPPOSITE   Villa Chiesina, a private villa in traditional Tuscan style, seen across the infinity pool and surrounded by lush vegetation and trees.

TUSCANY
ITALY

166

ABOVE   Reached via a winding track, Castello di Vicarello is perched on top of a hill overlooking the stunningly verdant Maremma countryside.

ABOVE In summer, dining al fresco on the terrace is a must. In colder months, guests dine in a stylish stone-paved solarium off the family kitchen.

ABOVE Generous communal spaces are furnished with leather club chairs, velvet-upholstered sofas, and a wealth of reading matter.

ingredients that come almost exclusively from the property: fruits and vegetables from the garden, eggs from the chicken house, wild game from the estate, and meat and cheese from local producers. Producing their own line of celebrated wines, Brando looks after 2.8 hectares (7 acres) of high-density, organically grown vineyards. For him, the ancient soil, rich in clay minerals, marine deposits, and calcium, is a testament that Tuscan history and traditions are nurturing grounds for the future.

ABOVE   The castle has a well-equipped kitchen for creating exquisite rustic, farm-to-table Tuscan meals. Many of the organic ingredients are grown on the estate.

MÁLAGA ANDALUSIA SPAIN

A New-Age Finca Where All Things Grow Naturally

FINCA
LA DONAIRA

At the heart of Andalusia, Finca La Donaira brings past, present, and future together in an eco retreat complete with an organic farm and equestrian center.

ANDALUSIA
SPAIN

ABOVE With its low-rise, thick, whitewashed walls, stone chimneys, and terra-cotta roof tiles, the *finca* is typical of vernacular farm architecture.

High in Andalusia's Serranía de Ronda, in southern Spain, Finca La Donaira is a shining example of luxury agritourism, a movement that combines farming and hospitality in the modern age. Set within 750 hectares (1,850 acres) of unspoiled terrain, and tucked between protected forests of ancient oaks and a biodynamic farm, at the heart of the property stands an old Spanish farmhouse with nine individually designed rooms for guests.

This Andalusian landscape is ancient. "Time seems to have slowed its course, the connection to seasons feels deeper," says retreat founder Manfred Bodner. In keeping with its surroundings, this traditional *cortijo* (Spanish for "farmhouse") has been painstakingly restored by local craftsmen over many years using traditional methods. A true labor of love, its architecture and interiors celebrate natural materials, ranging from stone floors and lime-plastered walls to tiled roofing, and interiors fitted with leather, wood, and copper. A rustic feeling permeates the house in its worn brown leather seats, wreaths of dried flowers, and exposed beams. The cortijo is surrounded by ancient oak trees, olive and almond groves, organic vegetable plots, and a vineyard. Scattered around are sheep, goats, rare-breed cattle, hens, and bees. Seventy Lusitano horses (the world's oldest saddle horse) roam freely on the land, bred and trained according to the principles of natural horsemanship.

Ahead of the sustainable curve, Finca La Donaira embraces the permaculture principles of farming, and has a medicinal garden based on the living pharmacies of medieval monastery gardens. Moreover, the biodynamic farm runs on the principles of Rudolf Steiner: "Our approach to farming is open and experimental," explains Manfred, "a mix of tradition and innovation all based on permaculture design principles." "Everyone has a connection to nature here: give guests something to look at, taste, or smell and you'll inspire them," adds Gerhard Bodner, Manfred's brother, a classical ballet dancer turned head gardener at the *finca* (Spanish for "country estate"). When Gerhard chose gardening over the stage some eight years ago, he imagined a vast garden focused on the 100 medicinal plants and herbs he deemed most important. "I have been so taken by this project, the intelligence of the plants, the knowledge of gardeners and botanists around the domain, that this garden is bigger and brighter than I could have ever dreamed," he explains. "Once you start taking care of plants, they thrive; it's impressive." While there are challenges to working in such an arid, mountainous terrain, his garden flourishes. Daily, Gerhard creates flower arrangements for the guests' rooms

ABOVE While all nine rooms at the *finca* are unique, each is rendered in a neutral palette of wood, leather, natural textiles, and white linens.

ANDALUSIA
SPAIN

ABOVE   Looking down on the farmhouse, which nestles comfortably on a gentle Andalusian hillside landscaped with terraces to the rear and vineyards and olive groves beyond.

ANDALUSIA
SPAIN

TOP AND ABOVE   The stylish interior of one of two yurts set within the *finca's* grounds.

ABOVE   The dining table set with homegrown and locally sourced products.

and offers guided walks through his planted pharmacopeia. "We have more than 300 different varieties of medicinal plants today, some of which end up in the kitchen, such as thyme with a menthol aroma and garlic from the Incas, which has a saffron edge to it. The marigold lemoni, which has a tutti-frutti flavor, we use for kombucha," he explains. Local gardeners' insights helped bring fruit trees into the garden, which provide shade for other plants, along with delicious nectarines, plums, peaches, apples, pears, and citrus fruits for the kitchen and guests alike.

In the kitchen, Swedish chef Fredrik Andersson, has led the finca's unique approach for four years: "I love the freedom of working here, and the challenges it brings. This is far more than a job; it means working daily with the land, the produce, the gardeners, while constantly pleasing guests," says Fredrik. "The food we prepare is the expression of a self-sustainable approach, to see how much we can create with what we have. We want guests to be moved by the taste of the land, by the expert yet simple expression of a raw material," he concludes. Fredrik loves sharing his craft with chefs from the neighboring pueblos. Together, they use techniques to bring out the best of local produce, whether that is leaving it raw, covering it in salt, using a *papillote*, or slow-cooking it for long hours. In addition, they forage for ingredients, collecting wild herbs, mushrooms, and wild rose pepper depending on the season.

With a view of experimenting with local potential, a trained psychologist recently reached out to Finca La Donaira. Passionate about donkeys and their natural grounding aura, she has since joined the team to offer guests walks and meditative experiences with the donkeys in the forest. "Our logo happens to be a donkey, so imagine how thrilled I was!" explains Manfred. "We have 12 donkeys on the estate, plus five births this year, and we encourage guests to spend time with them. We even organize for them to head out with a donkey to explore the domain; we give them a blanket and a packed lunch. The animal's grounding energy does the rest!"

Intent on looking forward while retaining its connection to the earth, Finca La Donaira runs the Soil Academy, which hosts talks from thinkers from all walks of life—natural beekeepers, rammed-earth architects, bird nest designers, influential farmers, and artists among them. "Our next dream is to develop a village with a primary school and nursery, for young kids," says Manfred. "We want to design a curriculum around permaculture for children. We want to have artists and scientists in residence and to build more rooms for staff. At the heart of this new project is the ambition to create a new retreat focusing on regenerating health; with a transgenerational approach, it would generate hundreds of new jobs."

This is a project designed to enrich the place that it is from, with longevity and community at its heart. "I hope that one day someone will take care of La Donaira; that they will bring it to the next generation," says Manfred. "This project is designed to outlive me."

Quinta da Côrte

Timeless Traditions Revived in the Douro Valley

TABUAÇO
|
DOURO
|
PORTUGAL

Set in one of the world's oldest wine regions, Quinta da Côrte is a historic estate that has been turned into an artful property, respectful of local traditions.

Scattered around the Douro Valley, quintas—historic Portuguese winery estates—have stood the test of time, with whitewashed walls, maroon tiles, and ancient olive trees marking out boundary lines. Quinta da Côrte is no exception: once forgotten, this 19th-century guesthouse has been turned into a 12-room inn by businessman Philippe Austruy, with the help of interior architect Pierre Yovanovitch. Although completely renovated in 2013, the guesthouse and its annexes retain the nostalgic elegance of the property's faded history. "I wanted guests to feel as if they were in a winemaker's house," explains Pierre. "The decor is based on rurality, on a local way of life, on the importance of the terroir and local crafts—on simplicity really. I wanted to invite life in with all its flaws: the main house needed to feel domestic, so we installed a central open fireplace in the kitchen." With contributions from local artisans, the design includes ceramics, terra-cotta floors, and azulejos—painted, decorative ceramic tiles. "Terra-cotta brings you back to the earth," continues the interior architect. "It highlights the importance of being surrounded by a terroir and different qualities of soil that artisans and winemakers equally work with."

Pierre and his team also sourced artisanal and agrarian-inspired artifacts and objects to complete the interiors: handwoven natural rugs, off-white plaster finishes, elegant rustic jars, rattan furniture, and vintage pieces that recall a different way of life.

OPPOSITE   The 19th-century casa at the heart of the Quinta da Côrte estate is typical of the region's vernacular farm architecture, with thick, whitewashed walls and wooden shutters.

DOURO
PORTUGAL

ABOVE The *quinta* is perched high in the hills above the Douro River, with its vineyard planted on terraces carved into the slopes below.

ABOVE   The interior design at Quinta da Côrte marries the traditional with the contemporary. Here a set of abstract tile designs grace the walls.

DOURO PORTUGAL

182

ABOVE   The crisp lines of the elegant, vaulted ceiling are married with inset stone paving and a contemporary metal staircase.

QUINTA DA CÔRTE

"Working on the *quinta*'s interiors brought back memories of my childhood when we spent summers in our family homes in the mountains or the countryside," says Pierre. "I remember the naive drawings on the tiles on the main table. They featured scenes of life and were very kitsch in a way, but they pictured life in Provence and it always felt like an escape." As a result, the artful tiles central to the Portuguese traditions were reinterpreted by Brittany-based artist Armelle Benoit to adorn tabletops in the main dining room.

The overall result is a muted feeling of sophistication that respects local agrarian traditions. Quinta da Côrte is fabulous but not loud, it is nostalgic and smart with references to history in a way that is thoroughly contemporary.

ABOVE   Styling is fairly minimal and furnishings are predominantly modern. In this dining space, cute sculptures occupy little niches in the walls.

Malhadinha Nova

A Stylish Rural Getaway Set on an Organic Farm and Vineyard

ALBERNOA
|
ALENTEJO
|
PORTUGAL

Set in Portugal's vast and open Alentejo region, where olive- and cork-oak-filled plains encompass all the eye can see, Malhadinha Nova tells a family story that revolves around wine. In 1983, Maria Antónia and João Soares opened a minimarket in Albufeira and, soon after, their first wine shop. The two evolved into a very successful wine distribution company, now operated by the couple's sons João and Paulo.

The entrepreneurial family then bought the 450-hectare (1,110-acre) Herdade da Malhadinha Nova estate, with the intention of running it as a winery with a traditional family home at its center. Twenty years in the making, the family home and values remain, the wines flow, and the Malhadinha Nova estate has become a vast sustainable farm and unique hospitality destination.

One after another, six ruined buildings were renovated and transformed into airy, down-to-earth rooms and suites. They include a 10-bedroom farmhouse, the Monte da Peceguina country house, timeless architectural suites Casa das Pedras, the slow-living villa Casa da Ribeira, the terra-cotta-hued Casa do Ancoradouro, and the two-bedroom Arts and Crafts house.

Interiors overseen by Rita Soares feature an elegant mix of Alentejan antiques and straw chairs, bespoke artisanal ceramics, an exclusive Malhadinha crockery line by Vista Alegre, locally baked clay tiles, and modern design pieces, all putting a modern twist on rural traditions. Outside, the vineyards and cork and holm oaks line the horizon, while Portuguese Lusitano horses, Alentejana cows, Iberian black pigs, and merino sheep remind guests of the authentic

OPPOSITE   The estate is surrounded by miles of sun-drenched plains dotted with olive trees. On the land that has been cultivated, pristine rows of vines stretch into the distance.

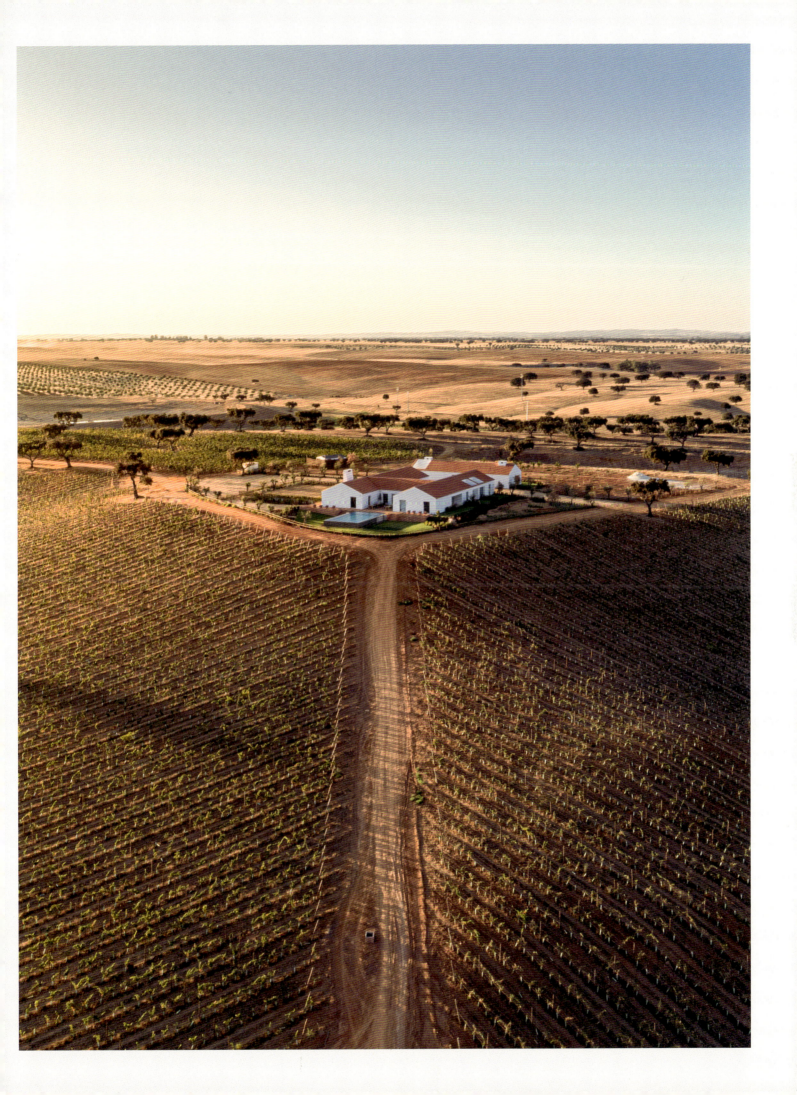

ALENTEJO
PORTUGAL

186

ABOVE AND OPPOSITE (TOP)   The rooms are furnished with timeless classics and rurally inspired artisanal pieces. Large windows provide a constant reminder of the world outside.

Alentejo way of life. In addition to their acclaimed wines—for which the Soares children draw labels in thick crayons featuring zebras, freckled cows, and bunches of grapes—the estate also produces organic goods from the family's olive groves, orchards, beehives, and vegetable gardens.

Offering a slice of rural Alentejo, the family strives to offer guests a creative field-to-fork culinary experience. Directed by Lisbon-based chef Joachim Koerper, the restaurant turns the estate's prodigious produce into unforgettable meals that include home-raised beef tartare, Malhadinha lamb with zucchini tart and rosemary from the herb garden, and cakes made using the farm's lemons. Guests walk back to their rooms under starry skies, where silence is golden and nature simply follows its course.

ABOVE   In the restaurant, exquisite food based on regional dishes is created using the freshest organic ingredients from the estate's fields, vineyard, olive grove, and pastures.

Metohi Kindelis

A Venetian-Ottoman Mansion Turned into an Organic Haven

CHANIA | CRETE | GREECE

Enclosed in a magnificent Mediterranean garden, Metohi Kindelis represents a journey through time. Echoing Crete's rich past, the property was first built during the Venetian occupation of Crete, as a summer residence surrounded by lush gardens. In the 17th century, during the Ottoman occupation, it was converted into a metohi—which is derived from a Greek word which means "monastic estate"—introducing a participative form of farming that continued successfully in the following centuries. In the Kindeli family for a hundred years, the estate's organic vegetable garden and orchards, plus three unique houses transformed to welcome guests for a luxurious rural experience, are run by third-generation Manolis Kindeli and fourth-generation Danai Kindeli.

A true visionary, Manolis has been a pioneer of organic agriculture in Greece since the 1990s: today, the 3.5-hectare (8.6-acre) estate grows oranges, bitter oranges, Egyptian limes, kumquats, mangoes, avocados, and lychees, and produces heirloom Cretan vegetables. Protecting the property's historical rural heritage, Manolis also decided to revive the estate's old olive oil press. After years of traveling the world for EU institutions and fashion magazines, Danai's sharp, creative eye settled on Crete. Her beautifully curated wabi-sabi interiors seem straight out of a film set. Think: a cracked rural platter heavy with oranges, an old gramophone, an elegantly modern handrail attached to an antique stone staircase leading up to a mezzanine room and a vintage trunk, all bathed in chiaroscuro. The kitchen area is stocked with fresh goat's cheese, olives, bread, almonds, fresh orange juice, and a manual coffee grinder. In the courtyard, where giant cactuses grow

OPPOSITE   The characteristic exterior of the farmhouse, with its arched doorways, and a Venetian-style red color that is now faded by time.

ABOVE   Much of the original architecture of the farmhouse has been preserved, with exposed stone walls, rough timber beams, and Venetian arches.

against raspberry-colored walls, a small shop sells a line of clothes Danai designed and beautifully sculpted objects out of olive wood. Staged like this, timelessness is a joy.

The three restored guesthouses respect both the character and the unique elements of the Venetian architecture: "We want [this] to be and feel like a Mediterranean family retreat secluded away in lush gardens. We never think of the estate as a hotel. We want guests to feel at home, explore the garden, taste the products, ask questions about the architecture, go on an archaeological tour, and explore Cretan traditions," explains Danai.

ABOVE Housed on the first floor of the farmhouse, the Kynthia guesthouse overlooks its own private, stone-paved yard with a majestic palm tree and a swimming pool.

Rural Traditions, the New Way Forward

By reenacting the past and celebrating local traditions, these locations invite guests to join them as they craft the present.

Living and breathing their chosen locations, a new generation of rural hoteliers is putting up a strong defense for local culture and tradition. By honoring and engaging with local customs, these new rurals are keeping them alive and inviting their guests to participate actively themselves. At the heart of any stay, culture-driven experiences encourage guests to forage, cook, mend, or learn about vernacular traditions through architecture and design.

"We wanted to honor local traditions, offer guests, locals, and visitors alike the opportunity to take dressage classes, ride in the vineyard, or enroll for a jumping session," explains Rita Soares, speaking from arid and rugged Alentejo, Portugal, a place where culture runs deep. Led by the Soares family, Malhadinha Nova is a 450-hectare (1,110-acre) estate with a luxuriously renovated farmhouse that acts as accommodations, and a stud farm that breeds Lusitano horses. The world's oldest saddle horse, the Lusitano was domesticated 15,000 years ago in the southwest of the Iberian Peninsula, which covers parts of southern Spain and Portugal. Loved by the ancient Romans, the poet Virgil referred to them as "Sons of the Wind."

With only a few thousand remaining, the importance of the Lusitano is intrinsic to Iberian culture. Taking over the estate in 2008, breeding pure-blood Lusitano horses was a dream that the Soares family wanted to share with many. Working with Pedro Sousa, who specializes in breaking in and training horses, the equestrian farm, which started with six mares and one stallion, now counts 32 horses. A handful of them have even made it to dressage competitions. Today, guests can take a dressage class, enjoy a ride, or simply learn more about this special breed.

Committed to protecting ancient Alentejan culture, the Soares family also organizes workshops that focus on specific crafts and lesser-known customs: they range from "Alentejano" singing with viola accompaniment to traditional dances, *bunho* weaving (an ancestral technique using a native reed), artisanal boot-making, and clay pottery. All represent the richness of the local rural traditions.

Andalusia, in southern Spain, is another region with an equine history that extends back across time and is rich with colors, costumes, and a unique choreography. In an effort to revive the equestrian history of the area, Manfred Bodner opened Finca La Donaira, a one-of-a-kind hotel that welcomes guests and also raises Lusitano horses. At La Donaira, guests are invited to meet with the horse whisperer, to engage in dialogue with the horses, and ride them across the rolling hills.

Like-minded rural hospitality venues all around the world are run with respect for traditions in mind. Active on many fronts, whether

ABOVE At Finca La Donaira in Andalusia, southern Spain, guests can ride Lusitano horses bred and trained at a stud farm on the estate.

architectural, relating to design and craft, or preserving natural richness (or all of them), embracing the local environment is at the heart of a project. For most of them, the respect for traditional or vernacular architecture is key. At Parco dei Sesi on the volcanic island of Pantelleria, Sicily, Margot Guelfi remembers being stunned by the specificity and beauty of the architecture: "The houses have one-meter thick lava stone walls, which we kept during the renovation. As we discovered that the island is rich in volcanic rock and sand, we teamed up with local builders to only use these materials. We learned from them that a homemade microcement was traditionally laid in between the blocks. Usually, it is used on outside terraces, but we applied it inside," Margot explains, insisting on the importance of respecting historic materials to blend in on this protected part of the island. "Choosing the pattern and colors, we also had handmade tiles made specifically. We really like to empower craftsmanship or rely on local resources," adds Margot, who bought many vintage objects from the Palermo auction house.

Preserving historical architecture, interiors, and objects was also key for art historian Bettina Klein when she took over an 1840s manor house and turned it into the Kranich Museum & Hotel in Germany. The museum building was renovated by a team of artists and builders, who revealed layers of history: elements of a 19th-century manor, East German postwar social housing, and present-day

ABOVE AND RIGHT The horses at Finca La Donaira are trained to compete in classical dressage. The estate calls on experts in the field to help develop training techniques for both horses and riders.

architecture coincide. Today, with six galleries and an artist residency program, the estate and park offer visitors a rare artful and architectural experience. "We hope to welcome locals, vacationers, and art lovers from the region and Berlin through our doors. As the first of its kind in the area, and indeed in the world, we are sure that it will prove popular," says Bettina.

Another strong proponent of craftsmanship, star interior architect Pierre Yovanovitch interacted with many artisans during the renovation of Quinta da Côrte's 19th-century residence overlooking the Douro Valley, one of Portugal's oldest wine regions, and known for its refined lifestyle. "Here, artisans and farmers have a way with the earth and the local terroir: they work with it in many different ways, to grow wines, or to craft *azulejos* (traditional ceramic tiles), or pottery items. We collaborated with a local artisan to produce custom-designed azulejos for the interiors of the guesthouse. Traditionally, every locality informs the patterns of the azulejos. They are always the same and never quite the same," Pierre adds, impressed by the deep relationship to the land local craftsmen have kept.

Other conscious hoteliers celebrate their site's deep relationship to the land and take steps to preserve the local biodiversity. Big in the Nordic countries, foraging is an expert science, one that requires great knowledge and comprehension of the natural surroundings. Launched by chef René Redzepi, the VILD MAD ("Wild Food") program connects people to nature and the landscape. "We want to teach people of all ages to read the landscape to discover its culinary potential— how to identify what is edible, how to harvest, how to cook what you find, and how to take care of nature while foraging," adds the man who is also behind the restaurant Noma and the

ABOVE Parco dei Sesi sits at the heart of an archaeological park, its luxury rooms set within original dammuso houses built from black volcanic rock.

Nordic food revolution. "Imagine if kids were able to stroll through the wild and pluck things like we do off supermarket shelves? If our kids are enriched by nature, if they see how much we depend upon it, and if they grow up loving it, then they will fight to take care of it," exalts the visionary chef.

In the footsteps of the Danish chef, the new rurals are keen to reconnect with the local wilderness, to fight for biodiversity, and to share their knowledge—and discoveries—with guests. Outside the kitchen at Stelor, on the Swedish island of Gotland, chef Linus Ström takes long walks to discover the richness of the land and brings natural delicacies back for guests to try. At Ebbio, Tuscany, Sibilla de Vuono forages year-round, bringing additional surprises to the table such as porcini mushrooms, chanterelles, asparagus, or stinging nettles in season. "I had no idea at the beginning you could forage so much," she says. "I had to learn to read nature, revert to old sayings, and question farmers. Mushroom areas were usually kept as family secrets: you can only start foraging when you become a local, or at least know the land like one."

Also fighting to preserve biodiversity and share her knowledge, beekeeper Paula Carnell helped create The Newt in Somerset's Beezantium. Through the bee safaris she organizes, guests and visitors discover the estate's colonies of rare, native, and wild bees, and learn more about their fascinating behaviors. Inside the Beezantium, bee habitats and working hives are integrated into the walls. "Sharing knowledge and educating visitors are key steps in helping them grasp the importance of biodiversity," says Paula.

A rare project, Bruno Cheuvreux set up an oak arboretum at Domaine de la Trigalière to protect and study 800 different varieties of oak trees from different corners of the world. "My goal is to create an oak conservatory with a scientific, educational, and environmental purpose that present and future generations can engage with," explains Bruno. "It's part of the estate's legacy: like we preserve old architecture and traditions, century-old trees should also be protected. Can you imagine a world without oaks? With climate change, they are going to have to adapt, and the more we anticipate, the better."

Led by the Garin clan, L'Auberge de La Maison is a perfect example of how vernacular architecture,

ABOVE At the Kranich Museum & Hotel, the rooms in both the hotel and the museum have been meticulously stripped back, layer by layer, to reveal the worlds of times gone by.

LOCAL TRADITIONS

TOP, LEFT AND RIGHT   Pierre Yovanovitch's creative renovation at Quinta da Côrte.

BOTTOM   At Deplar Farm in Iceland, local birds are mounted on the wall in the communal dining room.

ABOVE, LEFT AND TOP   Guests can learn all there is to know about bees inside the Beezantium at The Newt in Somerset, UK.

LEFT   Reading matter in one of the rooms at Guardswell Farm in Perthshire, Scotland, where everything produced by the farm is cultivated with circularity in mind.

timeless craft, regional recipes, and local villagers come together under one roof. Iconic, the family-run property is a slice of Courmayeur's history at the foot of Mont Blanc, in France, a place where legendary Alpine stories are born. In the lounge area, where the walls are covered in ancient oil paintings, Alessandra Garin talks about the latest book published on the Auberge: "We named it *Building the Past, Remembering the Future*," she explains. "We should always have in mind where we come from to find our way into the future. Traditions here are long lived; they act as an eye-opener and perfect guide into our fast-changing world. They hold most of the answers to today's questions."

LOCAL TRADITIONS

TOP   Living the slow life at Captains Rest in Tasmania, Australia.

BOTTOM   At Domaine de la Trigalière in Ambillou, France, guests are encouraged to reconnect to nature and their childhood memories.

Villa Lena

Agritourism Meets Artist Residency at Villa Lena

PALAIA | TUSCANY | ITALY

"I always tell my staff: imagine every client is your favorite grandma," says Lena Evstafieva, who left the art world to turn a late-19th-century villa into a not-for-profit hotel and artists' haven.

High in the rolling hills of Tuscany, Italy, Villa Lena is an agriturismo destination set among 500 hectares (1,235 acres) of woodland, vineyards, olive groves, and organic vegetable gardens, complete with converted historic agricultural buildings—former farmhouses, stables, and hunting lodges—that welcome guests and artists alike. "I never had a vision or desire to be in the hospitality industry," explains Lena. "I wasn't trained for it. I wanted to create a place where all people could interact seamlessly, find their own rhythm, explore, retreat." Each month, a handful of international artists take up residency alongside in-house guests, offering workshops and often leaving behind a work for the hotel, turning Villa Lena into an ever-changing gallery. Moreover, resident artists are encouraged to collaborate with the local Tuscan community.

At Villa Lena, 75 percent of the food served is produced on the estate. From the bread to the olive oil and sparkling rosé wine, everything offered is of Tuscan origin, sourced through local producers when not available on the property. "I am very passionate about sustainability," explains Lena. "We rely heavily on local artisans and materials and refrain from importing anything from outside. For example, we didn't buy any new furniture during the renovation, and found ways to upcycle." Each time a building is renovated, it becomes a green building, well insulated and frugal in energy consumption. And renovations seem to be endless on

OPPOSITE The handsome facade of the neoclassical-style villa at the heart of the estate. Artists taking part in the summer residencies stay in rooms inside the house.

TUSCANY
ITALY

TOP AND ABOVE RIGHT   With wooden floors and simple furnishings beneath vaulted ceilings, the rooms at Villa Lena are the epitome of understated elegance.

the extensive property. Gardener Gigi, known as the "orto man" also takes center stage. A botanist by trade, he tends the 2 hectares (5 acres) of vegetable gardens that supply the farm-to-table restaurant.

"Mostly, agriculture is about trial and error. There are so many variables, it is not an exact science," muses Lena. "We grow the best radishes but can't grow good carrots. Irises bloom and peonies die. We just keep on trying, learning, and adapting. We took a big leap forward when we installed solar panels and started recycling water for irrigation. And I never thought we would have a 40-square-meter (430-square-foot) worm farm dedicated to composting and generating natural fertilizers!" At Villa Lena, artist residencies, creative stays, and agritourism have redefined the Tuscan landscape.

ABOVE   Work in progress in one of the artists' studios. Each residency program lasts four to five weeks, during which artists are invited to attend talks and workshops.

TUSCANY
ITALY

204

ABOVE   Special farm-to-table feasts and wild-dining experiences in woodlands behind the villa are among the many shared treasures at Villa Lena.

TOP Produce growing in "the orto," the 2-hectare (5-acre) vegetable garden.

BOTTOM Recipes are simple, allowing the homegrown foods to speak for themselves.

Casa Balandra

An Artist Residency with a Community Feel

PÒRTOL
|
MALLORCA
|
SPAIN

Set on the Balearic island of Mallorca, in the small town of Pòrtol famed for its long-standing pottery tradition, Casa Balandra is a creative residency for up to six guests at a time. Designed as a place to share, create, and celebrate conviviality, it was founded by two sisters, Isabella and Claudia del Olmo.

In Spanish, *balandra* refers to a small, elongated fishing boat with a single mast and two triangular sails, and this house encapsulates the idea of a boat that sails along, visiting and discovering different lands and cultures. Besides its six bedrooms, large kitchen, dining room, living room, and garden with swimming pool, Casa Balandra's unique feature is its six shared studio spaces. Having grown up in the house, the Olmo sisters wanted to build on their family legacy to provide a safe space for young and promising artists amid an atmosphere of living closer together and slowing down. "The feeling of community that is created when working side by side, cooking, eating together, and sharing a space is hard to explain," says Claudia. "I believe the impact that the residencies have on the artists and on their future work has much to do with the people they meet during their month here."

At Casa Balandra, the whole house functions as a free creative space. Hosting up to six artists per residency, it brings together creatives from different fields and encourages an open exchange of ideas and work. Created in collaboration with designer Cecile Denis, the interiors are timeless and creative. While keeping the traditional essence of the house with its whitewashed walls, furnishings reflect the family history with their unique personality and patina and

OPPOSITE Looking toward the house from the swimming pool. Guests are encouraged to make Casa Balandra their home during their stay.

ABOVE Communal mealtimes are convivial affairs, with all of the guests gathering together; such times serve as the perfect platform for the informal exchange of ideas.

ABOVE The Casa Balandra kitchen is a homey space where guests can join in with cooking for the group. All activities at the house are shared experiences.

are juxtaposed with minimalist elements that include thick natural rugs, terra-cotta pots, and local crafts. Adding to the charm are the ever-changing creative touches that arise from the guests themselves—prints, drawings, and installations. "The house is filled with donations from past residencies; we hope they inspire guests and future artists, continuing the dialogue with Mallorca's rural island culture," muses Claudia.

ABOVE   Bedrooms are filled with an eclectic mix of vintage pieces, trinkets found at flea markets, vacation souvenirs, and works from past artists.

Kranich Museum & Hotel

A Historic Manor House Turned into a Museum and Hotel

HESSENBURG / SAAL
|
MECKLENBURG-WESTERN POMERANIA
|
GERMANY

Nestled in among the farmlands of Hessenburg/Saal in northern Germany, Kranich Museum & Hotel is a one-of-a-kind destination that combines a museum, an eight-room hotel, and a café all under one roof. *Kranich* derives from the German word for "crane," and the hotel is named for the hundreds of birds that stop by in the old trees and fields that surround the hotel as they make their twice-yearly migratory flight between Spain and Sweden.

The renovation of what was once an 1840s aristocratic manor house was the work of art historian Bettina Klein. Following a 20-year stay in Japan, she fell in love with the run-down estate and bought it at an auction in 1999. Conservation of the original, now dilapidated, building was key, and Bettina garnered aid and support from the village authorities and the local community. In line with her vision, American architect and artist Alex Schweder worked hard to keep fragments of the interiors that had accumulated over the years—paint layers, for example—while adding modern interventions to the historic structures. Importantly, Alex chose not to separate the museum from the hotel.

Today, the museum and hotel areas are integrated: all around the house, walls and ceilings bear traces of history and carefully curated historical furnishings create a tension between old and new. Six individually designed suites of varying sizes occupy the ground floor, with an additional two on the top floor; the museum rooms are located above and below. In addition to the eight suites in the main building, there are two apartments in a house on the grounds. The grounds themselves—a 5-hectare (12-acre) neo-baroque park—were revitalized in stages by landscape architect Ludivine Gragy.

OPPOSITE Collections at the museum center on works of contemporary art that are inspired by the house, its surrounding landscape, and their joint history.

MECKLENBURG–WESTERN POMERANIA
GERMANY

ABOVE   In the hotel, as in the museum, walls have been carefully stripped back to reveal the bare brickwork, although patches of the original plaster remain here and there.

KRANICH MUSEUM & HOTEL

Since the opening of Kranich Museum & Hotel in 2011, Bettina has invited artists to participate in an artist-in-residence program. Through performative work or installations on-site, they engage with the house, its architecture, surroundings, and history. Each new art object naturally becomes part of Kranich Museum's collection with associated documented material being exhibited in the hotel rooms to provide insight into the artistic process. Never has the frontier between museum and hotel been so fluid and engaging.

TOP   The apartments at the hotel are generous spaces with en suite bathrooms. Some have kitchen facilities and a bedroom in the loft; some have wood-burning stoves.

ABOVE   Looking toward Kranich Museum & Hotel from across the grounds. Since it opened, the vast brick building has become a respected local landmark.

Vipp Farmhouse

A Danish Farmhouse Embraces Nordic Design

SØLLESTED
|
LOLLAND
|
DENMARK

You can hardly see the building for all the trees, but take a closer look and you will spot the whitewashed walls and thatched roof of the traditional Danish farmhouse dating from 1775. Located on the island of Lolland in the Baltic Sea, the building is owned by the family-run design brand Vipp. Nestled in the forest on a 566-hectare (1,400-acre) estate, this former gardener's residence now features Scandinavian interiors respectful of the house's past. The ideal rural getaway for a family or friends, it can accommodate up to six guests.

Commissioned by Vipp and the estate owner Ulrik Th. Jørgensen, interior designer Julie Cloos Mølsgaard has created a modern farmhouse that combines nostalgia with modern convenience. From the wooden beams and imperfect furniture to natural rugs, vintage baskets, ceramic jars, and vases, everything is set for an enjoyable farmstay. The first floor opens up to a terrace garden, endless fields, and leafy forest views, while the upper levels overlook the surrounding countryside. "During lockdown, most of us rediscovered nature and the charm of the Danish countryside. There was a need to escape, to get a taste of farm life," explains Jette Egelund, second-generation Vipp owner, who also transformed a former industrial building called the Chimney House in Copenhagen.

For Vipp, building a hotel portfolio is about consuming less and experiencing more. "Today, the retail economy has become boring. If you consume great-quality products, designed for a lifetime, you automatically buy less and less," explains Jette. "If you consume products of lesser quality, you tend to forget the experience and even the product. Moving

OPPOSITE   The sun rises on another day at the Vipp Farmhouse. So meticulous was the external renovation of the original building that it has changed little in almost 250 years.

ABOVE   The architects preserved existing structural features, such as the exposed timber beams, and paired them with contemporary stone flooring and furnishings.

away from products to connect with nature and rural values, one lives to share quality moments: those are emotions that stay."

Naturally, the Vipp Farmhouse has a vast, central, fully equipped kitchen designed for cooking and hosting. Beyond the door, the surrounding estate is a botanical haven where endless discoveries await. As Jette believes, "Wonderful experiences are all you want to collect, cherish, and share in life."

ABOVE   While the farmhouse maintains its rural, rustic atmosphere, the rooms have been kitted out with modern appliances and a sophisticated monochromatic decor.

Almières

A Historic French Hamlet for Rest and Retreat

LOZÈRE
|
OCCITANIE
|
FRANCE

Set on a high plateau named Causse de Sauveterre, in one of France's remotest areas, the hamlet of Almières dates back to the 18th century. Here, old stone houses with thick walls and built-in water tanks stand alongside a communal bread oven and sheep pens, all crafted many centuries ago to help the locals see through the region's rough winters.

Carved with deep canyons, this mountainous landscape has recently joined the UNESCO World Heritage List for its agropastoral culture. Transhumance, the seasonal movement of livestock, is still practiced here in the traditional way, using the *drailles* (old stone pathways) that lead to the high plateaus. Steeped in silence and perfectly timeless, Almières' stone houses are surrounded by 8 hectares (20 acres) of exceptional land overlooking the 500-meter (1,640-foot) deep Gorges du Tarn.

Enamored with the ancient traditions and landscape of Almières, Marise Dematté, a former executive in a printing company, and Monia Senoussi, a music therapist passionate about yoga, bought the property in 2017. It took them four years to fully renovate the 1,000-square-meter (10,765-square-foot) hamlet and transform it into a mindful retreat. Devoid of internet connection, digital interference, and visual pollution, Almières welcomes guests to one of its four suites, the small shared house, or the lodge for five-day immersive stays practicing yoga, experiencing new sounds, healing, and regaining a clear mind.

Devotees of sustainability, well-being, and authenticity, the owners have installed bio switches and shielded ducts to avoid electromagnetic fields and to

OPPOSITE   Much of the appeal of staying at Almières is the timelessness of its buildings, with their rough stone walls and worn roof tiles.

OCCITANIE
FRANCE

224

ABOVE   At Almières, guests are encouraged to practice yoga outside, allowing them to become fully immersed in their natural surroundings.

OCCITANIE
FRANCE

ABOVE Old meets new in the communal spaces. Large window sections bring natural daylight into the cavernous rooms with their stone walls.

guarantee guests a deep and restful sleep. The duo worked with local artisans to restore the stone roofs, whitewashed the interiors with lime, and used a vegetal mix of cotton, linen, and hemp for insulation.

With no details left to chance in the creation of this perfect regenerative retreat, Marise and Monia sourced furniture and clay pots locally and bought artisanal French mattresses to increase a sense of place. During a stay, yoga and meditation classes alternate with healing treatments, energetic massages, and sound baths. At the end of each day, guests can attend workshops on naturopathy, Ayurveda, or the understanding of medicinal plants, and dine on vegan and organic cuisine. At Almières, everything is very much "alive," designed to be lived in the present moment.

ABOVE   All of the rooms at Almières preserve the architecture of the original buildings and are decorated in colors that echo those of the rugged Gorges du Tarn.

Eremito

An Eco Retreat with Monasterial Overtones

PARRANO
|
UMBRIA
|
ITALY

Perched atop a secluded hill in the heart of Umbria, Italy, Eremito is a modern-day monastery, built in recent times to capture the essence of the region's spiritual past. An eco resort for up to 14 guests, Eremito offers a unique escape for solo travelers seeking yoga sessions and a digital detox within its stone walls, and encourages them to embrace the benefits of solitude and quietness.

Umbria was the birthplace of Saint Francis of Assisi. Considered a spiritual focal point thanks to wonderful monasteries and the first Benedictine monks, it makes for a fitting choice for this natural retreat. Somewhat austere in appearance, the stone mansion overlooks a pristine valley and is surrounded by 3,000 hectares (7,400 acres) of rural terrain. Access is via a winding dirt road that climbs steeply toward the end, isolating the refuge from the dramas of the world outside.

Inside this spiritual stronghold, 14 individual *celluzze*, or room cells, are named after monks and saints. Each measures 9 square meters (100 square feet) and is loosely based on monastic cells of old: simple, but impeccably designed, each features a desk and chair carved out of the soft stone. Beds are dressed in traditional hemp-yarn sheets—not particularly soft, but aesthetically perfect. Simple light fittings are the work of artisans. Yet, the true focus is elsewhere: Eremito encourages guests to start their day in the chapel and to read or resource spiritually through meditation. This is followed by detoxifying walks in the woods, to the river or the waterfall, or simply in the garden. A stroll through the farmhouse is also an option, where an orchard, a herb garden, vineyards, and neat rows of fresh vegetables are plentiful. Handpicked daily,

OPPOSITE The approach to Eremito is a steep, winding track. Although newly built, the hilltop eco resort could have been standing on this spot for centuries.

ABOVE AND OPPOSITE (BOTTOM) Vaulted ceilings above candlelit rooms, flagstone floors, exposed stone walls, and long arched corridors evoke the spirit of an age-old monastery.

these are the main ingredients of the vegetarian food served at mealtimes. Inspired by ancient monastic traditions, each meal is eaten in silence: conversations at the dinner table are banned, leaving room for Gregorian chants and time for quiet contemplation. After that, guests are invited to wind down further in the refuge's vaulted communal spaces with their roaring fireplaces and vintage kilim rugs on the floor.

TOP   In winter months, meals are served in the refectory. The menu is vegetarian, with an emphasis on Mediterranean recipes and herbal teas.

A Sense of Place in Rural Areas

Often remote, picture-perfect, and hidden in nature, rural retreats convey a unique sense of authenticity and place.

On the lookout for a unique, enchanting place where nature still feels genuine, many people are choosing to settle outside urban centers in places where the idea of locality has not been destroyed by external forces or the homogenizing squeeze of globalization. Up a hill, tucked in a clearing, secluded on an island, the people behind new rural retreats hide away to craft a world of their own, and in doing so, are revisiting the very definition of hospitality.

"In 2017, we decided that we would build a house in the woods and invite all of you in. We hope you'll take off your coat, join us around the table, and stay a while," say Elizabeth Starks and Jacob Sackett, the owners of Bovina Farm & Fermentory in the Catskills, New York, USA. Now permanently set up in the mountain range a couple of hours' drive from the Big Apple, they have swapped the city life for one of farming and hospitality. In Germany, Anna-Dina and Sebastian Priller did something similar, trading a busy life in Augsburg for Ansitz Hohenegg, an Allgäu farmhouse from the 1700s that has been thoughtfully converted into a series of vacation apartments. Further south, Margot Guelfi and Massimiliano Panseca left the fashion world for Parco dei Sesi, a hotel settled within the volcanic landscape of Pantelleria, a small island off the Sicilian coast.

The stories of these hoteliers and guesthouse owners are always unique, but in them we see the significance of the place revealed. What is it about such rural locations that draws us to them? Is it because authenticity and wilderness prevail, and a sense of freedom still exists? For many new hoteliers, remote locations act as a protective shield and a blank page to start from.

In his book *Le sacre de l'authenticité* (*The Consecration of Authenticity*), philosopher Gilles Lipovetsky talks about the need for hotel professionals to value the genuine in people and in nature. He writes that people want to reconnect with natural landscapes and their rural heritage, to learn about biodiversity and wilderness. Destinations with nature that feels "intact," where human impact is less obvious, are celebrated because they are sources of pleasure that offer unique, long-lasting—sometimes even life-changing—experiences. As Lipovetsky explains, "Sustainability has definitely impacted the way we assess destinations: today, desirability comes from remote, wild, or extreme areas. Guests want to reunite with a self-sustaining world. The further away from industrialized work, the better."

What has clearly changed is the way a smaller, rural hospitality sector has moved to protect and embrace its environment while catering to a new kind of guest who is similarly interested in their surroundings. This new movement in hospitality, and those who are leading it "impact each and every stay through the

ABOVE At Refuge de la Traye in Les Allues, France, 13 chalets of varying size and functionality have been designed to look and feel like a traditional Savoie hamlet.

ABOVE Time stands still in the olive grove at Masseria Calderisi in Puglia, Italy, where trees with gnarled trunks have seen summers go by for centuries.

deep connection to the land, knowledge, and humanist values they carry," writes Lipovetsky. "With the guests, they share a sense of responsibility, which in turn, creates lasting change."

Embracing authenticity and a genuine connection to the land, these people differ from explorers in that they are not after pristine wilderness, they value arable lands, a balanced terroir, and the presence of knowledgeable people around them. Though they venture into the wild to forage, hike, or retreat momentarily, their daily lives revolve around their location. The new rurals are connected to the seasons through their gardens, farms, and animals, and to their community through dialogue with their friends, neighbors, and local producers.

This way of life, and the romance associated with it, is not new. Throughout history, people have traveled to rural locations for respite from the stress of cities, hoping mountain air or a sea breeze might heal their ailments or inspire them to make great art. Reenacting this holiday idyll, new rural hoteliers and business owners are bringing these "forgotten" regions forward, breathing new life into old buildings and embracing a different pace of life. Keen to reconcile past and present, they revive old techniques and grains, vintage furniture and textiles, heirloom vegetables and tools, and take great pleasure in revisiting recipes and crafts from the past.

To protect regional identity, as expressed through traditional architecture and crafts, a new guard of rural hoteliers is teaming up with local architects, builders, and artisans to create buildings that are true to place. In the pages of this book, you will find small hotels and guesthouses that were once barns, sheds, distilleries, and farmhouses. There are contemporary spaces and modernist cabins and even a half-Ottoman, half-Venetian mansion. Each project has been thoughtfully created with place in mind, either through restoration and transformation or designed and built from scratch. This book celebrates their audacity.

Many have chosen to be bold in the reimagination of historical buildings, finding ways to repair vernacular detailing and fighting to protect local heritage and building techniques. On the island of Pico in the Azores, former advertising professional Benedita Branco transformed the island's abandoned, dilapidated distillery into a six-room boutique hotel, Adega do Fogo. The black telluric stones that compose the walls are pieces of the island's rich volcanic and winemaking history. Inside Refuge de la Traye's Alpine chalets, exposed ceiling beams convey a long tradition of woodwork and the importance of skilled carpenters in the Alps. The renovation of the property would not have been possible without the valley's expert craftsmen. Vernacular architecture is an art form. In the south of France, Marise Dematté and Monia Senoussi transformed a

ABOVE   In Puglia, a region affectionately known as the farm of Italy, new rurals at Masseria Calderisi are keen to uphold regional customs and to celebrate the locale's regional produce.

CLOCKWISE FROM TOP LEFT   Village retreat in Crillon-le-Brave, France; Tasmanian lakeside fisherman's shack Captains Rest; lakeside cabin and forest trails at Nimmo Bay, Canada.

centuries-old farm into the comfortable and chic Almières. When repairing the ancient stone roof, the pair discovered that there were only a handful of artisans with the skills required for the job.

Through their courageous undertakings, these new hoteliers are able to align the past and present of their locations. In Portugal, José António Uva, who runs Barrocal—an 800-hectare (20,000-acre) farm with accommodations—explains that renovations need to be done in a sustainable way, but that "sustainability can't be a sum-up of certifications, checklists, and consulting firm validations that follow protocols with set variables. You need to be much more pragmatic in this arid part of the country. I have found that sustainability is what is passed down from generation to generation. It sustains life on a broader timeline, bringing together the past, the present, and the future." In this part of Portugal, it is said that you should plant vines for yourself, olive trees for your children, and cork trees for your grandchildren. A wise vision.

Looking at rural destinations, new hotels, and farmstays, it is striking to see the ways in which regions stand out. It is less about Canada than it is about Newfoundland, less about New York than it is about the Hudson Valley and the Catskills. The same can also be said of Italy, Greece, Portugal, Germany, Sweden, and Norway.

Such regional development has been possible thanks to greater connectivity. Today, relocation to a small town outside of an urban center does not have to

TOP   Sheep graze on a grass rooftop at Deplar Farm, Iceland.

BOTTOM   Come nighttime, guests are treated to the northern lights.

be a daydream. Leaving the city is not as daunting as it used to be. Working remotely, setting up a small business, gardening more instead of commuting, and paying cheaper rent means opportunities are easier to seize for young professionals and families. In their book *Campagne (Coming Home to Nature)*, authors Estelle Marandon, Gesa Hansen, and Charlotte Huguet talk about a "new rural art de vivre," a guide to curating a happier life away from urban centers. "When we left the city for the countryside, we were prepared to be bored, to miss the stores open at all hours, our local coffee shop, or cinema. But once there, it's surprising how little we missed. It simply brews down to essential needs," they say.

Day after day, they noticed that a different relationship to the elements comes into play, like the presence of the sky and the vast horizon (which seems so much bigger than in cities), nature's perpetual movement, and the change of light and seasons. Then, having a larger home means it is possible to invite friends, think bigger, and be more inclusive. And things crescendo. Rural living means beauty is not delivered to your door in the form of a trending object or the latest outfit; it comes from functional pieces and immediate pleasures, like picking an apple and eating it under the tree. "Countryside living is also humbling," says Charlotte. "It's also about learning and sometimes the hard way. Learning to water the garden, to change a spare part, or fix the house. But in the end, it gives you a unique sense of belonging. You know you are in the right place, exactly where you should be. And that, along with nature's soothing presence, is most reassuring."

BOTTOM Exploring Murgia National Park by bike during a stay at Sextantio in Matera, Italy.

TOP Guardswell Farm, Perthshire, Scotland.

A SENSE OF PLACE

TOP AND LEFT   Life at Adega do Fogo in São Roque do Pico in the Azores is infused with the history of Pico island's namesake volcano.

ABOVE   The architects preserved existing structural features, such as the exposed timber beams, and paired them with contemporary stone flooring.

Adega do Fogo

A Former Distillery Transformed into a Small, Volcanic Hotel

PICO ISLAND
|
AZORES
|
PORTUGAL

Having once served as a distillery on Pico island in the Azores, today Adega do Fogo is a boutique hotel with accommodations and dining facilities for up to 12 people. Surrounded by dark lava stones and ancient vineyards, the hotel stands overlooking Mount Pico, Portugal's tallest mountain. The volcanic giant rises some 2,350 meters (7,700 feet) above sea level and has influenced activity on the islands for many centuries. Testimony to its nutrient-rich soils, hundreds of thousands of singular vines enclosed in stone *currais*, or clusters, are among the island's incredible UNESCO-listed landscapes.

The hotel is the creation of former advertising professional Benedita Branco, who first visited the site in 2017. On seeing the dilapidated former distillery, Benedita was drawn 200 years back in time and, wanting to reconnect with history, she set about renovating the run-down building to preserve its heritage. Today, behind the original facade, and with interiors designed by Ana Trancoso, Adega do Fogo welcomes the past and celebrates local crafts. Features include bespoke furniture made of chestnut wood, restored beams, and woven light fixtures. Black stone indentations in white walls are reminiscent of the original walls.

Modest and soulful, the interiors reconnect with the building's agricultural past. Even the communal distillery has been brought back to life—it had once been one of the main distilleries on the island, used by locals to produce liqueurs and brandy. Today, its restored stills produce homemade *água ardente* using ingredients from the island—Pico bananas, pineapple, Irish strawberries, and sweet potatoes. During production (from November through February) guests

OPPOSITE Looking across the pool at Adega do Fogo toward a communal living room where guests can gather to spend time together.

AZORES
PORTUGAL

ABOVE   The six rooms at Adega do Fogo are bright and airy, with exposed beams and timber floors. The black lava stone is ever-present in feature walls and window frames.

ADEGA DO FOGO

243

can participate in the making, thus perpetuating long-lived island traditions. Days at Adega do Fogo can also be spent learning traditional songs, attending workshops making butter and baking cornbread, fishing, or joining wine-tastings under the towering presence of Mount Pico.

ABOVE   Whether lounging by the pool with views of the volcano (top) or finding a shady spot among the old stone *currais*, guests have numerous places to enjoy their natural surroundings.

AZORES
PORTUGAL

244

ABOVE Dominating the view, Mount Pico rises in the distance, a fitting reminder of the role the volcano has played in the island's heritage.

ADEGA DO FOGO

245

Eumelia

A Naturally Abundant Greek Retreat

LACONIA
|
PELOPONNESE
|
GREECE

Set in the Laconia region of the Peloponnese, Greece, Eumelia is an organic farm that welcomes daily visitors for olive oil tastings, wine tastings, farm-to-table cooking classes, and harvests in season. With five self-catering houses for those who want to stay overnight, it has become the epitome of Greek agritourism.

Owner Frangiskos Karelas gave up an international career to return to Greece and run his family estate, which includes more than one thousand olive trees, turning it into an eco-friendly rural retreat in the process. With unbridled vision and passion, Frangiskos traded degrees in economics for permaculture diplomas and trained to become a certified wine, olive oil, and olive sommelier. Rethinking the estate, he planted hundreds of fruit trees and endless rows of vines, introduced farm animals, and established vegetable gardens and herb plots based on regenerative and biodynamic principles. "Helping nature regenerate and respecting local communities are a priority at Eumelia," claims Frangiskos. To achieve this goal, eco-friendly materials, bioclimatic architecture, geothermal power, eco-technologies, and clever composting and water recycling were used in setting up the retreat, and continue to keep Eumelia both ecological and green.

Inspired by traditional Greek farmhouse architecture, Eumelia's five self-catering houses were designed to bring guests closer to the Greek farming landscape. Each one has a bedroom, a living room with a dining area, a fireplace, and a fully equipped kitchen, plus a large veranda that spills out into a private garden, which itself opens onto the ancient olive grove and the surrounding mountainous landscape.

OPPOSITE Planted in the Greek farming landscape, the guesthouses are named for the flora most associated with the farm: grapevines, olive trees, almond trees, lavender, and sunflowers.

ABOVE All five guesthouses follow the same model and are painted in a dusty red so that they are in harmony with the red earth of the local terrain.

EUMELIA

Enjoying local produce and traditions is also key here. The farm's culinary tour includes venturing into the gardens to pick vegetables and cooking farm-to-table meals; discovering local recipes and their culinary history; tasting natural wines; and learning about olive oil and its health benefits. A stay here also offers a chance to dance to ancient rhythms, traveling to ancient Laconian archaeological sites and historical monuments far from the crowds.

ABOVE A selection of fresh produce from the farm: melons, eggplants, and bell peppers.

TOP Looking out across the olive grove and to the mountains beyond.

Captains Rest

A Heritage Fishing Shack Brought Back to Life

STRAHAN
|
TASMANIA
|
AUSTRALIA

Perched beside a lake on Tasmania's wild west coast, Captains Rest is the ultimate tranquil oasis. Available as short-stay accommodations with Airbnb, this renovated fishing shack attracts guests seeking a rural getaway. With a pier and small fishing boats nearby, it invites all who stay here to head right out and connect with the elements. The result is an immersive stay amid the island's world heritage forests, close to the sea.

The shack's serene ambiance lies in stark contrast to owner Sarah Andrews' journey in creating Captains Rest. In 2012, the former scientist was sailing alone in the Pacific Ocean, off the coast of Mexico, when a storm rolled in and shipwrecked her. This humble, Tasmanian fishing shack became Sarah's refuge, bringing respite from the busy modern world while she transitioned from a life at sea to one back on land.

Little by little, Sarah renovated the heritage-listed fishing shack from the floor up—a project that took time, resilience, and effort, given that the nearest hardware store was eight hours away and the shack was in a terrible state of disrepair. Heritage shacks like this are a common site in the region. Constructed in the 1940s out of disused lightweight building material at a time when the area was only accessible by steam train, the remote shacks were intended not as permanent homes, but rather for seasonal, recreational use. With Sarah's labor of love, Captains Rest has become a carefully curated place to decompress, escape from a busy life, and slow down. The experience can be truly transformative. A stay at Captains Rest allows guests to travel back in time. Antique oil paintings inspired by Sarah's mother's collection line the walls, rustic windows

OPPOSITE   Looking toward Captains Rest from the lake. The whole scene is one of tranquility and comfort within the natural surroundings.

TASMANIA AUSTRALIA

ABOVE   Inside the shack, rooms are small, with dark timber floors, whitewashed walls, and large windows with stunning views across the lake.

ABOVE Two sofas face each other in a cozy corner of the shack beneath bare bulbs suspended from the ceiling and atmospheric oil paintings on the walls.

TASMANIA AUSTRALIA

254

ABOVE The kitchen is basic, with a wooden countertop, shuttered windows, and the minimum of appliances. Every inch of the shack reflects the simplicity of rural living.

frame the outdoors reality, and old brass lamps and furniture lend the interiors a traditional vibe. Even modern additions, such as the deep green cushions, were stitched by Sarah's parents, retired upholsters, using vintage velvet that Sarah had been hoarding for years. "Here, everything has a place. It's about slow, the best of everything, and only just enough," concludes Sarah wistfully.

ABOVE Owner Sarah Andrews' finishing touches emphasize that life is slow here—a collection of books to read, a rope for mooring the boat, and blankets for long winter nights.

BOTIZA   MARAMUREŞ   ROMANIA

A Project Committed to Sustainability and Local Traditions in Romania

ŞESURI

Set on a 100-hectare (245-acre) estate in the northwestern Carpathian Mountains of Romania, Şesuri comprises a handful of traditionally built houses, a farm, and countless animals.

There was never a plan to create Șesuri. When Volker Bulitta and Lilli Steier ventured out to Romania for long weeks of hiking back in the 1990s, they had never heard of the valley of Maramureș, even less so the village of Botiza. But it was Botiza that changed their lives and they, in return, have changed the fortune of the village and villagers through a project committed to heritage and community.

A paradise found, Șesuri today is a rural retreat that rents traditional houses, celebrates nature, rural traditions, old construction techniques, and local crafts. Working with local carpenters and farmers, Șesuri thrives on this very special relationship to time that locals have. "No doubt, this is an enchanted corner of the world, and mine is quite the dream job!" Steier explains. "I'm really grateful. I couldn't have found a better fit and place in my life; it brings so many facets together: construction, woodworking, sharing passions, learning from others, caring for nature and animals. All things I love seem to have come together."

When the pair first visited Romania from Germany, the country's remote regions were monetarily poor. The wildflower-covered hills they hiked through were home to people living in harmony with nature, leading a life of hard work that—to the outsider—seemed untouched by time. In and around their wooden houses, built without nails or screws, they made baskets, spun wool, wove carpets, raised livestock, kept bees, and grew organic crops in organic fields. In these remote regions there seemed to be almost no need for money because the land gave the people all they could want.

That is what they felt when they crossed the Botiza valley in 1998. Hit by bad weather, they decided to stay overnight in the village. "We were touched by our hosts' hospitality and on the last day, we left our business card in case they ever needed anything," the couple says, not realizing such a call might change their lives. Five years later, the phone rang: a child from the village had eye cancer and the only place she could get treatment was Germany. Overnight, Volker found the right hospital in Essen and one week later Florica Sidau and her daughter Maria arrived, greeted by Volker and a translator. The family stayed with Lilli and Volker for the five months of treatment, forming a lasting bond.

That year, Lilli and Volker were invited to spend Christmas in Botiza. The following year, Carmen and Vasile Trifoi, Florica's sister and brother-in-law, extended an invitation and asked the couple to spend the summer with them. Long days, great hikes, and a few beers later, Vasile suggested the couple should buy a holiday house in the village. As they were about to leave the country, they saw an old house in ruins in a neighboring village. They shook hands with the owner only to come back the year later, in 2005, to purchase it. Șesuri was born.

"This is how it all started, and we had no idea back then where it would lead us," the couple concedes. Now 17 years later, Șesuri totals five traditional houses, with another currently under construction, plus a barn with an apartment; it has a farm with Carpathian horses, highland cattle, goats, chickens, and beehives, as well as workshops and a foundation. To keep its operations running smoothly, Șesuri employs 16 people from the village.

"Our business has grown from renting a house to agriculture and now to bespoke furniture making," says Volker proudly. A trained joiner who later studied interior design, Lilli comes from a family of carpenters and architects. She is the driving force behind Șesuri's exemplary architecture and bespoke furniture. Each house on the property is an old local ruin that has been dismantled, repaired, and reassembled on a new plot of land. "With Volker and the help of friends from Botiza, we identify and buy the ruins. Vasile takes a building down, numbering the pieces one by one like a puzzle; wooden pieces are checked, repaired or changed using old parts, and treated naturally. Once the new drystone foundations are ready, all elements are transferred and a new roof put on with proper insulation," Lilli explains. In just a few days, the new house is up: "Alert and professional, Vasile and his team have done it many times; they are keeping tradition alive."

Taking over, Lilli then slightly modifies the interior plans, to change a doorway or eliminate a wall, for example. Traditionally, the houses relied on a ground floor only, as the upper floor was used to store grains. At Șesuri, all houses have two floors: two bedrooms and a bathroom upstairs, and a kitchen, living room, bathroom, and library downstairs. The interiors are fitted with a mix of bespoke furniture and vintage objects chosen by the couple. A second system is in place alongside, which sees Lili working hand in hand with a team of local carpenters to design bespoke furniture in oak for clientele across Europe. "We were all so proud when we shipped pieces to our first German clients," she recalls, "especially Ioan, who started working with us when he was 17 years old." Ioan Roib is a master furniture maker and carpenter—"the village's best asset," according to Lilli. Working together and learning from one another are key to Șesuri's success.

It was with this mindset that the couple set up the Botiza Foundation, an NGO that aims at improving

TOP   All of the properties at Șesuri have stunning views across the Maramureș countryside.

BOTTOM   Great efforts have been made to create authentic, homey interiors filled with antiques, regional curiosities, and local crafts.

ABOVE   Casa Cătuna, traditionally plastered with loam and painted blue, sits in a meadow with cherry, plum, and apple trees. Beside it stands a traditionally furnished barn.

MARAMUREȘ
ROMANIA

TOP   A quiet sitting room, tucked away beneath the eaves at Casa Mari.

BOTTOM   Kitchens are filled with flea-market crockery, glasses, and utensils.

ȘESURI

the general living conditions of the people in Botiza through its program of ecological, social, and cultural projects. "We don't want Șesuri or Botiza to become museums, we want traditions to be lived in, and accessible to all in the present," says Volker, humbled by the couple's journey. "After so many years, it still feels like a fairy tale: we wake up every morning wondering if it's true."

TOP   Among the livestock at Șesuri are Highland cattle (pictured) and Huculs, a robust horse breed of the Carpathian Mountains.

Guardswell Farm

A Family Farm Built to Last

PERTHSHIRE
|
SCOTLAND
|
UK

Set within 60 hectares (150 acres) of grassland, Guardswell Farm in Scotland offers panoramic views extending from north of Dundee, along the Tay River, and over to the north of Fife. At the heart of the property, a former farmhouse renovated to sleep 10 offers the perfect rural escape for guests, who are encouraged to embrace nature as well as a host of activities the venue has to offer.

The farmhouse lies at the heart of the farm's greater ecosystem: "Everything at Guardswell—our accommodations, our team and family, our workshops and events—feeds off our land and the greater surrounding community," explain the Lamotte and Wilson families, who have been overseeing the estate since 2011. For Guardswell is a family story that dates back to great-grandmother Nana, who founded one of Scotland's first milk bars at Inveralmond, and grandfather Robert, who went from growing herbs in his farmhouse to supplying restaurants across the United Kingdom. Respectful of the local terrain and rejecting chemicals, the family clans build and grow everything from the soil up with circularity in mind: organic nutritious vegetables are sold year-round, fresh grass and golden hay feed the Hebridean sheep and angora goats, and conservation grazing of the meadows is put in place to increase biodiversity and regenerate the soils. As a result, every day, Guardswell Grows—a regenerative, chemical-free market garden set inside a repurposed horse-van—sells homegrown vegetables and herbs to guests, visitors, and the local community. "We're by no means perfect, and we have a long way to go! But we pay attention to the heirloom seeds and the peat-free compost, the timing of the sheep

OPPOSITE   One of several cabins on the farm, the Infield is totally off-grid and boasts incredible views over the Scottish landscape.

ABOVE The Kailyard cabin is a modern take on a shepherd's hut, snugly fitted with a double bed, a wood-burning stove, and a small kitchen.

ABOVE   Approaching Guardswell Farm along a wooded path. This secret getaway is perfect for guests looking to immerse themselves in simple, bygone ways.

on the meadow at the end of summer, and the leaving of fallen trees for microorganisms," the Lamotte and Wilson families explain.

Staying on the farm means committing to this eco-considered, design-led, digital-free, and locally sourced way of life. Cozy with lots of wood cladding, soft sheepskins, and exceptional views, the one-bedroom cabins are scattered on the hillside and furnished with rural artifacts, local artwork, wooden furniture, and crisp white linens. Those who book also have the opportunity to learn new skills in masterclasses and workshops on such diverse subjects as miso fermentation, spoon carving, and botanical skincare.

ABOVE All the creature comforts are here for slow living: a wood-burning stove, cozy sheepskin throws, and plenty of books.

Deplar Farm

A Luxury Outpost Set on a Former Sheep Farm Embraces Icelandic Nature

FLJÓT VALLEY
|
TROLL PENINSULA
|
ICELAND

Set on an 18th-century sheep farm in Fljót Valley on northern Iceland's mountainous Troll Peninsula, Deplar Farm is a luxury-lifestyle outpost with 13 suites offering a unique gateway for nature lovers. The old farm sign still stands at its entrance and, although fully converted, the farmhouse maintains much of its humble character. From a distance, the picture-perfect building stands timeless, resistant to modernity.

Surrounded by towering, snow-dusted mountains and emerald-green pastures, the Deplar Farm was acquired by Eleven Experience, along with several thousand acres of adjoining land. In renovating the building, they drew on local sources for materials and services, which include natural stone from nearby rivers and geothermal energy. An elongated grass-covered roof runs the length of the dark timber building, helping it blend into the natural landscape and a geothermally heated indoor-outdoor pool erases boundaries between lodge and valley. Once inside, floor-to-ceiling windows maximize the views of the surrounding peaks. Not too far away, Deplar Farm also owns two cabins along the Hölkna River in which guests can overnight even deeper into the pristine wilderness.

At the root of Eleven Experience's philosophy is the desire to help people get "off the beaten track," and to experience some of the world's most beautiful landscapes. "We scour the globe for destinations relatively unknown, with a strong connection to both community and landscape," explains American owner Chad Pike. The firm's aim is also to empower local communities through direct charitable activities, environmental outreach, and education. Deplar Farm,

OPPOSITE   Dwarfed by towering snow-covered mountains, Deplar Farm sits in a rugged and remote landscape. Guests get to appreciate the sheer scale of their natural surroundings.

TROLL PENINSULA
ICELAND

TOP   A conscious choice of building materials—blackened wood and a grass roof—ensures that the farm buildings have the least possible visual impact on their surroundings.

OPPOSITE (BOTTOM) AND ABOVE Although the farm buildings look rustic and traditional from outside, the generous interiors have a more contemporary feel.

TROLL PENINSULA
ICELAND

274

ABOVE   At Deplar Farm guests are encouraged to explore the abundant and breathtaking landscapes that surround the lodge, and to enjoy big, star-filled skies at night.

DEPLAR FARM

for example, helps to maintain a long tradition of horseback riding—the Troll Peninsula is considered the cradle of Icelandic horsemanship. As such, a stay at the farm offers a unique way of living aligned with traditions, rural culture, and the immediate natural environment.

TOP Guests staying at Deplar Farm can use spa facilities that include a geothermally heated indoor / outdoor pool, i-sopod floatation tanks, and an outdoor Viking sauna.

Fogo Island Inn

A Visionary Outpost Designed for the Local Community

JOE BATT'S ARM
|
NEWFOUNDLAND
|
CANADA

Located off the northeast coast of Newfoundland along Canada's Iceberg Alley, the wild and remote Fogo Island Inn has operated as a creative retreat since 2008. With 29 rooms and suites that look out across the Atlantic Ocean through floor-to-ceiling windows, the inn's mission is to invite artists, filmmakers, writers, musicians, curators, designers, and thinkers to do their research, produce visual and musical content, or simply create, inspired by the raw outdoors.

In these particular surroundings, the retreat would have little to offer without the vision of founder Zita Cobb. An island native, Zita works tirelessly to raise the profile of Fogo Island, to revitalize its rural surroundings, and to bolster its economic stability. She runs the inn through a charity and all of its income is reinvested in the community.

Fogo Island Inn was designed by Newfoundland-born architect Todd Saunders. Striking in its appearance, the building represents his futuristic interpretation of local outport architecture: "I wanted to find 'new ways with old things,'" explains Todd. Traditionally, outport settlers were not permitted to build permanent structures or dwellings, and this led to the creation of temporary wooden structures built on stilts. "The vernacular architecture inspired me to create this centerpiece, which evokes local traditions while embracing modern contemporary design," he adds. Inside the inn, rooms blend the richness of local tradition with the very best of contemporary design. "Centuries of geographic isolation forced Fogo Islanders to become masters of making things by hand, recycling, and drawing on local resources

OPPOSITE   Todd Saunders' carefully considered building rises on stilts above the island's craggy rocks. On the upper floor, the dining room cantilevers out over the waves.

NEWFOUNDLAND
CANADA

ABOVE   Guests at Fogo Island Inn have more than 200 kilometers (125 miles) of paths, routes, and trails through untamed wilderness to explore.

NEWFOUNDLAND CANADA

ABOVE In a room with ocean views, guests dine beneath chandeliers conceived by Dutch designer Frank Tjepkema, suspended from a dramatic vaulted ceiling.

FOGO ISLAND INN

281

to resolve challenges," explains Zita. Here, international designers worked side-by-side with Fogo Island's artisans and makers to create custom furniture and furnishings that hint at both the old and new worlds. Besides custom-designed wallpaper and brightly colored hooked mats, key furniture pieces such as Elaine Fortin's boat-inspired punt chair, Donna Wilson's plush Berta chair, and Ineke Hans' cushioned rocking chair, hint at the island's long-standing culture of fishermen, boatbuilders, and local artists, making this inn a standalone creative destination in itself.

ABOVE In a style the hotel describes as "handmade modern," bedrooms feature custom-made, organic, natural-fiber beds and locally crafted furniture and textiles.

Ilimanaq Lodge

A Tiny Settlement at the Edge of the World

DISKO BAY
|
QAASUITSUP
MUNICIPALITY
|
GREENLAND

A short boat ride from Ilulissat, Greenland's third-largest city, Ilimanaq Lodge lies in a small arctic settlement some 300 kilometers (185 miles) north of the polar circle. Comprising 15 contemporary cabins on the edge of the mountain, the lodge is surrounded by pristine nature and stunning views of Disko Bay, one of Greenland's most celebrated natural landmarks. It is not unusual to see an iceberg float by or to witness a family of whales swim by.

What makes Ilimanaq Lodge truly unique is its social dimension. In 2010, the village had more than 80 inhabitants, but this fell to around 50 in just one decade. In a bid to save the local community, to create jobs, and to embrace Greenlandic traditions, three parties joined forces to create this lodge. The local Qaasuitsup Municipality invested to improve village infrastructure, maritime conditions, and sanitation. The Danish foundation Realdania By & Byg restored two historic buildings on the site, preserving many of their original materials and colors. Two of Greenland's oldest manmade structures—a former home and shop—they date back to the 1700s and once belonged to the missionary Paul Egede, son of Hans Egede, founder of the Greenland colony. To complete the project, World of Greenland constructed the 15 cabins.

The combined expertise of the three parties has resulted in a lodge that speaks to the past, the present, and the future. At its heart, the two old buildings house the reception, a conference room, and a restaurant in which an original sail from a whaling ship hangs from the ceiling. Meanwhile, the new cabins are forward-thinking in terms of both design and

OPPOSITE Perched right on the edge of the craggy rocks, each of the 15 cabins has its own private terrace overlooking Disko Bay.

QAASUITSUP MUNICIPALITY
GREENLAND

ABOVE Looking down toward one of the cabins, across beautiful wild terrain. It really does feel like being at the edge of the world.

sustainability. Large windows take up their entire two-story facades, maximizing the views out to sea. They are also equipped with solar panels where any surplus electricity is sold to the settlement at a low price. Truly pioneering in its approach, Ilimanaq Lodge has taken Greenland's tourism industry to the next level.

ABOVE   The two original houses stand on both sides of a rugged road. Having braved the elements for almost 300 years, they have stood the test of time.

A

ADEGA DO FOGO
Pico island—Azores—Portugal
adegadofogo.com
Photography: Francisco Nogueira
pp. 239 (top and bottom left), 241–245

ALMIÈRES
Lozère—Occitanie—France
almieres.com
Photography: Eugeni Pons
pp. 223–227

ANSITZ HOHENEGG
Grünenbach im Allgäu—Bavaria—Germany
ansitz-hohenegg.de
Copyright Ansitz Hohenegg
Photography: Robert Kittel
pp. 97–101

AUBERGE DE LA MAISON
Courmayeur—Aosta Valley—Italy
aubergemaison.it/en/
Photography: Beatrice Pilotto
pp. 103, 133–137

B

BOVINA FARM & FERMENTORY
Bovina—New York—USA
bovinafarmfermentory.com
Photography: Christian Harder
pp. 121–125

C

CAPTAINS REST
Strahan—Tasmania—Australia
captainsrest.com
Photography: Lean Timms
pp. 2 (top right), 199 (bottom), 236 (top right), 251–255

CASA BALANDRA
Pòrtol—Mallorca—Spain
casabalandra.com
Photography: Guglielmo Profeti
pp. 106 (top left), 207–211

CASTELLO DI VICARELLO
Cinigiano—Tuscany—Italy
castellodivicarello.com
Photography: Elena Foresto
pp. 165–169

D

Daylesford Longhouse
Elevated Plains—Victoria—Australia
daylesfordlonghouse.com.au
Photography: Philip Huynh
pp. 140, 144, 145 (top and bottom right)

DEPLAR FARM
Fljót Valley—Troll Peninsula—Iceland
elevenexperience.com/deplar-farm-iceland-heli-skiing
Photos courtesy of Eleven Experience
pp. 5 (bottom), 197 (bottom), 237, 271–275

DEXAMENES SEASIDE HOTEL
Kourouta—Peloponnese—Greece
dexamenes.com
Architects: k-studio, www.k-studio.gr
Creator & owner: Nikos Karaflos
Photography: Claus Brechenmacher & Reiner Baumann Photography
pp. 27–31

DOMAINE DE LA TRIGALIÈRE
Ambillou—Touraine—France
domainedelatrigaliere.com
Photography: Benoit Linero
pp. 77–81, 199 (top)

DOMAINE LES BRUYÈRES
Gambais—Île-de-France—France
domainelesbruyeres.com
Photography: Virginie Garnier
pp. 153–157

DR. KAVVADIA'S ORGANIC FARM
Tzavros—Corfu—Greece
drkavvadia.com
Designed and created by Apostolos Porsanidis-Kavvadias
Photography: Markos Kyprianos
pp. 109, 159–163

E

EBBIO
Monteriggioni (Siena)—Tuscany—Italy
ebbio.it
Photography: Ricard Romain
Home styling: Sibilla de Vuono
pp. 107 (top), 111–115

EREMITO
Parrano—Umbria—Italy
eremito.com/en
Copyright Eremito
pp. 229–231

EUMELIA
Laconia—Peloponnese—Greece
eumelia.com
Copyright Eumelia
pp. 247–249

F

FINCA LA DONAIRA
Málaga—Andalusia—Spain
ladonaira.com
Copyright Finca La Donaira
pp. 170, 172–176, 193–194

FOGO ISLAND INN
Joe Batt's Arm—Newfoundland—Canada
fogoislandinn.ca
Photography: Alex Fradkin
pp. 105 (top), 277–281

G

GRACE & SAVOUR, HAMPTON MANOR
Hampton in Arden—Warwickshire—UK
hamptonmanor.com
Photography: Grace & Savour, Hampton Manor
pp. 83–87, 141 (bottom), 142 (top right)

GUARDSWELL FARM
Perthshire—Scotland—UK
guardswell.co.uk
Photography: Murray Orr
pp. 198 (bottom), 238 (top), 265–269

H

HECKFIELD PLACE
Heckfield—Hampshire—UK
heckfieldplace.com
Copyright Heckfield Place
pp. 3, 139, 142 (top left), 147–151

HOTEL CRILLON LE BRAVE
Vaucluse—Provence—France
crillonlebrave.com
Photography: Mr. Tripper
pp. 89–91
Photography: Yann Deret
p. 236 (top left)

I

ILIMANAQ LODGE
Disko Bay—Qaasuitsup Municipality—Greenland
worldofgreenland.com/en/ilimanaq-lodge/
Photography: Gustav Thuesen
pp. 283–284, 285 (bottom)
Photography: Lisa Burns
p. 285 (top)

INIS MEÁIN RESTAURANT & SUITES
Aran Islands—County Galway—Ireland
inismeain.com
Photography: Andy Haslam
pp. 63–65, 141 (top)

INNESS
Accord—New York—USA
inness.co
Photography: Adrian Gaut
pp. endpaper (front), 43, 45–47
Photography: Christian Harder
p. 44

K

KRANICH MUSEUM & HOTEL
Hessenburg/Saal—Mecklenburg-Western
Pomerania—Germany
kranichhotel.de/en/
Photography: Philipp Obkircher
pp. 196, 213–217

L

L'ARMANCETTE
Saint-Nicolas de Véroce—
Auvergne-Rhône-Alpes—France
armancette.com/en/
Copyright Armancette
pp. 117–119

L'OVELLA NEGRA MOUNTAIN LODGE
Inclès Valley—Andorra
lovellanegra.com
Copyright L'Ovella Negra
pp. 108, 127–131

LE MOULIN
Lourmarin—Provence—France
beaumier.com/en/properties/le-moulin-hotel/
Photography: Gaëlle Rapp Tronquit
pp. 21–25

M

MALHADINHA NOVA
Albernoa—Alentejo—Portugal
malhadinhanova.pt
Photography: David De Vleeschauwer
pp. 107 (bottom)
Photography: Fréderic Ducout
pp. 185, 187
Photography: João Guimarães
p. 186

MASSERIA CALDERISI
Fasano—Puglia—Italy
masseriacalderisi.com
Copyright Masseria Calderisi
pp. 4, 15–19, 142 (bottom), 234–235

METOHI KINDELIS
Chania—Crete—Greece
metohi-kindelis.gr
Photography: Danai Kindeli
pp. 189–191

MEZI PLŮTKY
Čeladná—Moravia-Silesia—Czech Republic
meziplutky.cz
Photography: Romana Bennet
pp. 93–95

MORGADO DO QUINTÃO
Lagoa—Algarve—Portugal
morgadodoquintao.pt
Copyright Morgado do Quintão
p. 2 (bottom)

N

NEST 13
Zarrentin am Schaalsee—
Mecklenburg-Western Pomerania—Germany
nest13.de
Copyright Nest 13
p. 2 (top left)

NIMMO BAY
Mackenzie Sound—British Columbia—Canada
nimmobay.com
Photography: Jeremy Koreski
pp. 5 (top), 104, 145 (bottom left),
236 (bottom)

P

PARCO DEI SESI
Pantelleria—Sicily—Italy
parcodeisesi.com
Photography: DEPASQUALE + MAFFINI
pp. 57–61, 195

Q

QUINTA DA CÔRTE
Tabuaço—Douro—Portugal
quintadacorte.com/en/
Photography: Christophe Goussard
pp. 180 (bottom), 181, 183, 197 (top)
Photography: Jean-Francois Joussaud
pp. 179, 180 (top), 182

R

REFUGE DE LA TRAYE
Les Allues—Savoie—France
refugedelatraye.com
Photography: Gilles Trillard
pp. 39–41, 233

ROSSO
Allgäu—Bavaria—Germany
dasrosso.com
Photography: Lisa Rühwald
pp. 74, 75 (top left)
Photography: Wim Jansen
pp. 73, 75 (top right and bottom)

S

ŞESURI
Botiza—Maramureş—Romania
sesuri.com/en/sesuri/
Photography: Sorin Morar
pp. 256, 259–263, endpaper (back)

SEXTANTIO
Matera—Basilicata—Italy
sextantio.it/en
Copyright Sextantio
pp. 238 (bottom), 239 (bottom right)

**STORFJORD HOTEL
AND OWNER'S CABIN**
Ålesund—Norway
storfjordhotel.com/en/
Photography: The Ingalls Photography
pp. 33, 34 (top)
Photography: Margaret M. de Lange
pp. 34 (bottom), 35
Photography: Selena Taylor
pp. 36–37

T

THE AGRARIAN KITCHEN
New Norfolk—Tasmania—Australia
theagrariankitchen.com
Photography: Luke Burgess
p. 143

THE NEWT IN SOMERSET
Burton—Somerset—UK
thenewtinsomerset.com
Copyright The Newt in Somerset
pp. 48, 51–55, 105 (bottom),
198 (top left, top right)

THE ROOSTER
Livadia Bay—Antiparos—Greece
theroosterantiparos.com
Styling: Anestis Michalis
Photography: Yiannis Rizomarkos
pp. 9–10
Photography: Mirto Iatropoulou
pp. 11, 13 (top)
Photography: Nick Nikolaou
p. 12
Photography: Clara le Fort
p. 13 (bottom)

TOURISTS
North Adams—Massachusetts—USA
touristswelcome.com
Copyright TOURISTS
pp. 67–71

V

VILLA LENA
Palaia—Tuscany—Italy
villa-lena.it
Photography: Lottie Hampson
pp. 106 (top right), 204, 205 (bottom)
Photography: Lottie Thompson
p. 106 (bottom)
Photography: Niklas Adrian Vindelev
p. 201
Photography: Henrik Lundell
p. 202 (top and bottom left)
Photography: Marina Denisova
p. 202 (bottom right)
Photography: Frederik Vercruysse
p. 203
Photography: Annabel Sougné
p. 205 (top)

VIPP FARMHOUSE
Søllested—Lolland—Denmark
vipp.com/en/hotels/vipp-farmhouse
Copyright Vipp Farmhouse
Photography: Anders Schønnemann
pp. 219–221

Slow Escapes
Rural Retreats for Conscious Travelers

CLARA LE FORT IS A FRENCH TRAVEL AND LIFESTYLE EDITOR.
SHE SPENDS MOST OF HER TIME TRAVELING TO UNSPOILED LOCATIONS
WHERE NATURE IS PRESERVED. SHE IS THE CO-EDITOR OF *SLOW ESCAPES*.

A SPECIAL THANK YOU TO GUILLAUME BURUCOA
FOR HIS UNCONDITIONAL SUPPORT,
TO BLANDINE CHAMBOST AND MARIE-CLÉMENCE BARBÉ-CONTI
FOR THEIR UNIQUE PRESENCE

This book was conceived and edited by gestalten.

Edited by Robert Klanten and Rosie Flanagan
Contributing Editor: Clara le Fort
Introduction and text written by Clara le Fort
Captions by Anna Southgate
Editorial Management by Anastasia Buryak

Design, layout, and cover design:
Lisa Reckeweg for Herburg Weiland, Munich
Layout assistance: Melanie Ullrich
Photo Editor: Francesca Zoe Paterniani

Typeface: Larish Alte by Radim Pesko
and Band Eins Sans by Formatpunktoft
Cover image: Ilimanaq Lodge.
Photography: Gustav Thuesen
Backcover image: Dexamenes Seaside Hotel.
Photography: Claus Brechenmacher &
Reiner Baumann Photography

Printed by Grafisches Centrum
Cuno GmbH & Co. KG, Calbe Made in Germany

Published by gestalten, Berlin 2022
ISBN 978-3-96704-075-3

© Die Gestalten Verlag GmbH & Co. KG, Berlin 2022

All rights reserved. No part of this publication may be reproduced or transmitted in any form or by any means, electronic or mechanical, including photocopy or any storage and retrieval system, without permission in writing from the publisher.

Respect copyrights, encourage creativity!

For more information, and to order books, please visit www.gestalten.com

Bibliographic information published by the Deutsche Nationalbibliothek. The Deutsche Nationalbibliothek lists this publication in the Deutsche Nationalbibliografie; detailed bibliographic data is available online at www.dnb.de

This book was printed on paper certified according to the standards of the FSC®.